Godfather Drosselmeier's Tears
& Other Poems

Other Books by Alexander Theroux

FICTION
Three Wogs
Darconville's Cat
An Adultery
Laura Warholic; or, The Sexual Intellectual

FABLES
The Schinocephalic Waif
The Great Wheadle Tragedy
Master Snickup's Cloak
Fables

SHORT FICTION
Early Stories
Later Stories

POETRY
The Lollipop Trollops and Other Poems
Collected Poems
Truisms

NONFICTION
The Primary Colors
The Secondary Colors
The Enigma of Al Capp
The Strange Case of Edward Gorey
Estonia: A Ramble Through the Periphery
The Grammar of Rock: Art and Artlessness in 20th Century Pop Lyrics
Einstein's Beets: An Examination of Food Phobias
Artists Whol Kill and Other Essays on Art

Alexander Theroux

§

Godfather Drosselmeier's Tears
& Other Poems

Tough Poets Press
Arlington, Massachusetts

Copyright © 2023 by Alexander Theroux.

Some of these poems first appeared in *Conjunctions* (online) and *The Rupture*.

Cover illustration copyright © 1988 by Edward Gorey, and used with permission from The Edward Gorey Charitable Trust.

ISBN 979-8-218-30152-1

Tough Poets Press
Arlington, Massachusetts 02476
U.S.A.
www.toughpoets.com

To Sarah,
Shenandoah, and Shiloh.
"Amor omnibus idem"
—Virgil

This collection gathers new poems all having been written over the years subsequent to the publication of my *Collected Poems* (2015). Of the variety of topics they address, I would by way of explanation point to Emily Dickinson's incorporating remark: "I dwell in possibility." The Amherst poet declared, "They say that God is everywhere, and yet we always think of Him as somewhat of a recluse." I daresay, an integral part of the possibilities she and I acknowledge is simply the process of seeking Him out.

A.T.

Contents

Godfather Drosselmeier's Tears	19
Horton's Radishes	34
West Barnstable Cemetery	36
Richard M. Nixon	38
Whither Went the Lad I Once Knew?	39
A Goodbye to a Baby's Great Betrayal	40
Why Sail to the Limberlost?	41
When Wee Shenandoah Chews and Bites a Popsicle	42
No One's Happier Than When He Holds a Handful of Flamingo	43
Mickey Mouse's Mug	44
Rhubarb Has a Voice	45
So Dear to My Heart Made Life Unreal For Me	46
Hosta Blue Cadet as a Civil War Memorial	47
All Crows Are Sentries	48
Real Estate Advisors	49
Dim Bulb	50
Henry Thoreau in His Garret at 225 Main St. Concord, Mass.	52
Poet and Peasant Overture	54
Catbriar	55
Shiloh and Shenny's Seawater Green Eyes	56
Hats	57
"Holiday for Strings"	58
Joshua Tree	60
J'Accuse	61
Asthma	62
Shiloh and Shenandoah Walking at 20 Months	63

Threnody from a Child	64
Flashback	65
The Day Augustus Saint-Gaudens Introduced Robert Louis Stevenson to General William Tecumseh Sherman in the Palace Hotel	66
"Deep Throat"	68
Abstract Expressionist Paintings Are Spat Out	69
Oh, Get on With It, For Heaven's Sake! or, the Fault of Films	72
Last Request	73
Shenandoah at Two Walks on Her Toes	74
Horseshoe Crab	75
Herring Gulls	76
Shiloh's Great Voices	78
A Cat Licking Africa	80
An Epithalamium for Peter Palandjian and Eliza Dushku, August 18, 2018	81
How to Climb a Sand Dune	82
Unde de Artesque	83
Suicide in Tenerife	84
Mannerberefts	85
The Bedruthan Steps	86
No True Hero Is Part of a Flock	87
North Dakota Tourist Home	88
Perennial Prejudice	89
Senator Ted Cruz's Face	90
The Man That Cannot Be Reached	92
At the Nedick's Stand in Old Herald Square	94
Shirley Temple's Salary	96
Wheatgrass Drink	97
Sexual Misconduct	98

Villa Islazul	101
Joseph and His Brethren	102
A Tiger's Stripes Are Flames	103
Captain William Bligh Never Had a Son, Fletcher Christian Never Knew His Father	104
Raymond Chandler's Women	106
The Desert Fathers	107
Bird of Paradise	108
His Cremains Will Be Inurned	109
Speaking of Ozymandias	110
Crane	111
I Was Looking for Me	112
Jehu the Madman	114
There Exists No Present	116
Mrs. Bindweed and the Poll Tax	117
Elision	119
Altered Offerings	120
Henry Thoreau and the Pine Tree	122
Stalin	123
Osprey Nest in West Barnstable	124
Toad	126
Please Don't Let It Be Gray	127
An Ex-friend E-mailer	129
Poppies in New England	130
Hansel and Rätsel	131
My Death by Hieronymus Bosch	132
The Sin of Wearing Periwigs	133
The Quality of Mercy	135
Anxiety at the Blue Mosque	136
Venomous Cone Shells	137

The Habit of Saying No	138
The 31st of August	140
An Alias Is a Mask of Pure Deceit, a Liar's Trope	141
Dragonflies in Autumn Wheel	143
Nervous Breakdown	144
Logion	146
Dick Nixon was an Endoproct	147
Toss Pot	148
Archbishop Talbot Blacklaws	149
I Shudder to See My Books Misaligned	151
Hyperborea	152
Heavy Rain Like Mah Jongg Tiles in Thailand	153
Stanley Pissoir Loved to Obey	154
Mermaid Hair	156
Poussin	157
Aural Symmetry	158
Panther Attack in Diyatalawa	159
Death Is Not An Event in Life	160
Nose Twisters	161
As I Rode My Bike from Carondelet	162
O, to Go Home, but Where? I Was Never There!	163
Islam Loves Sheepmeat	164
Mr. Wartofsky, the Antique Coin Dealer	165
The Responsibility of Owning Such a Face	167
Clive of Warninglid	169
Reflections on One's State	170
Table Mountain in Cape Town, South Africa	171
The Silversword Plant	172
Breaking Waves	173
John Profumo Cleaning Toilets at Toynbee Hall	174

I Love You the Way It Rains Diamonds on Jupiter	175
Capitalism	176
Time Is Money	177
Rhino the Gardener	178
King Louis XIV	179
An Old Ball Mason Teal-Blue Fruit Jar	180
Princess Grace of Monaco in the Rain	181
Honoré de Balzac	183
Asseroe in Ballyshannon	184
Logic and Truth	185
Parson Mullinex's Glebe	186
Cormorant	188
Four-Year-Olds Talk Like Laurel and Hardy	190
Conundrum	191
John Wayne Slings the Bullshit in *Red River*	192
Constant Is Neither the Nature of Wind	193
Mental Asylums Carry Terrifying Names	194
Le Ferte	196
Circularity of Mind	197
Larry Nassar the Pedophile	198
Dialogue of Self	200
Looking at Corot Landscapes in Widener Library on a Dark Rainy Afternoon	202
Fred Astaire and Latin Lovers	204
The Cranes of Binnalhyuk	205
Napoleon in Three Steps	207
Nectar for Pollen	208
The Unbranching of Reverend Hole	210
Who Would Deny the Well-Fed Warble?	212
Eutychus Raised from the Dead at Troas	213

Mr. Jessup	215
Woodpecker Drumming	218
Storge	219
Night of the Screech Owl	220
"Fuck Hate"	221
Rev. Billy Graham's Presumption	223
Flower Cookery	224
Farewell, Kind Friends, and Adieu	225
Slumberers Two (at Four)	226
Competing Pedals	227
Orange	228
On the Occasion of Angela Cormier's Engagement to Be Married	229
Legacy	230
Olga Scrapeshave	231
Trump of Doom	232
"I Thirst"	234
Was the Hermes Typewriter Made for Rant?	235
Annual and Perennial	237
The Sorrowful Rain of Contrition	238
Bad Dream	239
You Can Virtually Watch a Poppy Bloom	240
The Anthony ("Antimony") Stibnite Scholarship	241
Wind in a Copper Beech	242
Amy Lowell at Night	243
Hair Is Meant to Hide Behind	244
The Swing	245
Reading *The Lorax*	246
Henry Thoreau Fishing	247
Anthony Bourdain Commits Suicide	248
Opening an Envelope Begins a Pavane	250

Why Do Fat Italian Guys with Flourishes	251
The Roundness of Emily Dickinson	252
Henry Thoreau Sleeping under a Board	253
"Sympathetic Interviews"	254
Sapling Oak	255
Go Anywhere But Back	256
Early Meadow Rue	257
Death Is the True Beginning of Real Life	258
Authorize Appropriately	259
Song for Shiloh and Shenandoah	260
Fatal Gift	261
Henry Thoreau the Walker	262
Grandfather Herod, Son, and Grandson	264
Castaway	265
Phillips Andover Faculty	267
God Is Being	268
Glacier Ice	269
The Final U-Turn of Clara Bay Fingerhood	270
The Cycle of Willamette Sours	272
The Black Grapes of Calcotaggio	274
Shiloh and Shenandoah and The Doors	275
No Bird in the Hand, No Bush	276
Verecundia, the Punishment Whore	277
Henry Thoreau and His Lichen Repasts	278
Christ's Lineage Included Women Prostitutes	279
Appeasing Hannah Screecham	280
Nightmare	282
Winifred Pineweevil Who Never Shuts Up Talks All the Time	283
Cider Apples	284
Matthew 24:42–44	285

Jesus in Bethany	286
Rosa on a Bicycle	287
Fritz Haber Invented Poison Gas	288
Jump Rope Song	289
The Village Store, Mr. Woodshake, Prop.	290
Handsome Dan	295
St. Joan of Arc's Feast Day, May 30, Paris	296
Yahweh's Covenant with Israel	297
Henry Thoreau Loved Common Weeds	299
A Boulder Has a Brain of Sorts	301
Lament on a Deathbed	302
Dorothy Wrinch	303
Jews Fleeing Germany, 1943	304
Shenandoah, Age Four, in Crisis	305
Rosalie Pitou and the Cedar Tree	306
War in Afghanistan	308
Mrs. Quark and Her Kids	309
Katharine Hepburn	310
Jane Birkin and Serge Gainsbourg	312
A Body Is But Cobbled Plans	313
Effort Is Everything	314
The Beauty of America Is Its Space	316
Only When Kafka Was Ready to Die	317
John Singer Sargent	318
Father Pedophile	319
A Character Is a Part	320
Nelson Eddy, Kevin Costner, and Robert Taylor	321
Depend Upon a Zebra	322
Jody Arias	324
Reality	325

A Barking Mother Terrifies Her Young	326
Fame Sucking	327
Older Parents	328
Shipbuilder Oak	330
Judas	332
The Colors of Paul Bowles	333
Owlage	334
Pot Roast	335
Robert Frost Throwing Pennies	336
Departure Always Leaves a Hollow Freedom	337
Miss Hudnut's Trees	338
Reverend Stone Shallcross	340
Porcupines in the Trees	342
Twin Needles	343
Sugaring Time	344
The Delight in Being Wrong	345
Gannet Girl	346
White Cargo	348
Norma Jean Baker	349
Caruso Begrudged the City of Naples	350
One Never Sins for No Cause at All	352
Storms Make Me Feel Wonderful	353
Patriotism	354
1763	356
No One Can Ride Like the Blackfeet	357
Igbok Karatoprak Was a Noted Chiropractor	358
As I Go Walking in Paris, I Hear the Bells	359
Over a Lifetime I Have Eaten Ten Cows	360
No Photograph Can Ever Capture Duration	361
Chantal Destroismaisons	362

The Perennial Is Not the Eternal	363
Creation Is But a Part of the Majesty of God	364
Wicked Boy	365
Shiloh and Shenandoah at Age Five	367
Flammable Cladding	369
Sharp Leaves	371
Stalin Loved to Munch on Roasted Bear	372
Jesus in Egypt	374
Henry Thoreau Doesn't Become a Catholic	375
Drowned in Nova Scotia	376
Suicide Notes are Almost Always Inconsequential	377
Malfeasance	379
Shakespeare's Forests	380
Long Ago Is Far Away	381
Mrs. Komodo in Mid-Scream	382
Elias Pennebaker Hated Bitterns	384
Salem, 1692	396
Aiken Colcord's Tributary Meal	387
Henry Thoreau and the Wilderness	390
Antarctica	392
Watch the Skies	394
The LGTBQIA2S + Rag	395
God's Mother	396
Dead Alive	398
We All Die at the Perfect Moment	399
Culinary Christmas	400
Jocasta Hockey's Illness	401
Ethiopian Food	403
Bird Beaks	404
Merle Haggard Was a Wuss About His Mama	405

Stavrogin *et Cie*	407
A Trial of the Body Is a Test of the Soul	409
Big White Hunter	410
Movie Star	411
Tenement Stairs	412
Pink, Blue, Purple	414
Magnificent Sumo Wrestlers	416
Green Monster	417
Ghoulography	418
Wet Blankets	420
Greta Garbo	422
Twin	423
Limpet	424
Reverend Treat Is Laughing Again	426
Salt Herring	428
Go Away!	430
This Way to the Human Race	432
God Always Sees a Child Escapes a Massacre	433
Alistair Thumb and Alison Space	434
The Faces of Modigliani	436
Mrs. Stakeknife	437
The Judge with the Gerbil IQ	438
Asclepias Tuberosa	439
Martin Buber Steals the Jerusalem Family Home of the Writer Edward Said	440
Face of a Rose of Sharon	441
Easy It Didn't Was	442
To Morons Who Wastefully Leave Lights Burning	443
Indians of Arizona	444
There Exists That Rare Freedom	445

Godfather Drosselmeier's Tears

> "But, dear God, please give me some place, no
> matter how small, but let me know it and keep it."
> —Flannery O'Connor, in prayer

I who knew it badly wrong to quit a venture
when it became routine knew I'd do what Noël Coward
    would,
like any weak, neutral, yawning Laodicean,

and so big God, tall and eye-patched to avoid
having to watch my incorrigible fears and boiseried corruptions,
disordered, corrupt, larboard-leaning,

opened no goatbag of shiny gifts to me,
lest by pride and vanity I falsify the Scriptural pages I thumbed,
no wiser than a blunt-muzzled capybara,

figuring if Absalom was the handsomest
man in the Bible I would settle to be a knave of hearts, anything
remotely blessed, a squire with fox-red hair,

say, some pomeroy in a stiff collar and tie
allowed to arrive at some small certainty, raise an eyebrow or two,
not necessarily a soul to invent the wheel,

prove, for all my sad, workaday baseness,
that I merely be not *fooled* in this life, penalized by commonness,
be no fawning houseguest on this planet,

even if no tall apostle, a fool, yes, but a fool
to make a difference, somehow, to rise above the life I was handed,
some bravo to frivol with a little fire.

Tinfoil-hat alert: I asked God for more,
sharpening my quills and gathering reams of paper to write books
as a balancing antidote to all I was not!

I grew up in the loud, gabby anarchy
of a big family with four brothers and two sisters. We fishfaddled
into our busy teens like common beagles,

barking for food, playing out our fickle fates,
although for all stages of amazement I focused predominantly on
my wet, my lost, my bewildering childhood,

until I could take it no more, seeing finally
by way of my siblings' continence that my evil was not a problem
to be solved but rather a fate to be endured.

I loved my dear parents, Depression-children,
although I must confess I could have committed avunculicide
against one evil dwarf priest who abused me,

an uncle who mocked me for my bed-wetting
from about age six to ten, whenever he came to visit our house.
I feared this Abaddon, my mother's brother,

so much it ate up many of my waking speculations
as if they were the dry crackers I at some remove use to snap
in half, as if panfuriously splitting his soul in two.

I had not and never had the privilege of *certainty*,
that cool and effortless sense of high privilege born of wealth
and what is widely referred to as high breeding,

but convictions I did have, yes, a luminescence
close to genius, my mind no fish-paste factory with a slubbering
chum floor of dead smelts, fat cod, red porgies,

and I ever envisioned myself a muscular Federalist
wearing a black cockade. I loved and grew up in Massachusetts,
where revolution is native to soil and soul.

In early grades I dreamt I could hang my cloak
on a ray of sun and turn high clouds into a hundred horses, smiling
down at me, fast, as I galloped into whirlwinds

and in early classes invoked the angel Yasriel,
keeper of the seventy holy pencils, for inscribing the holy name
of the Lord I loved. At my old deal school desk

I felt close to the aeviternal, fully believing
modals like "could," "would," and "should" actively worked
for me, shinnying up my fate, with aspirations.

Later, in low, crepuscular *beuglants* over notebooks,
I sat smoking green pot for the scenic comfort of vegetable
    television,
and filling endless pages with truly nutty screed.

I had the option of picking a creature of the earth
as the dwelling place for my poor soul, and my spirit had chosen
the unattractive being that I am for residence

and vantage point. We choose our shells. For
any nobler quarters of life's accommodation I was never worthy,
my sinning soul quailing at a higher selected self.

My catechism shed dark light upon simple texts
of corruption in this world, the intrigues of energetic revengers,
all the Mulligrubs, Mendozas, and Malevoles

I'd come up against in life. "Hark, lust cries
for a surgeon, what news from limbo?" seemed to cover it all.
The cartoons I drew were funny but grim,

growing out of a slang I came easily to adopt
as a form of cultural democracy by way of comics but also books
of a richer sort my father read to us by candle,

classics like Stevenson and Edgar Poe, not hacks
like the Gabblers and Blotters and Scumblers from *Zit's Weekly*
and the *Daily Nooze*. "Ramp up, my genius,

be not retrograde!" I told myself with Jacobean
energy, as my imagination flamed high with fables, early radio,
an odd movie, my soul becoming a pied butterfly!

I saw authors in frilled collars on many a page
holding feather pens, a finger propping up their cheeks to ponder
character and plot and design and dimension.

A work of great art offers itself to everyone
but belongs finally to none, according to Baudelaire. It gives
itself away freely, indiscriminately, in the way

that any two-act ballet belongs to any boob
perched in any seat in any row in any theater he claims, and so
I secretly hoped that art and love, partaking

of the same self-surpassing generosity
through which God gives Himself to the world, might find me
myself worthy who would *also* co-create.

Wasn't I competent, clever enough to count,
show God I was not just another queer quidnunc in this world
a stupid rubber chew toy, a right prat?

I who in my searches was able to discern
terpsichorean warp in a thunderstorm, scarlet-eyed cvoirths
among angels, maleks, and moody messengers,

sought God by joining the holy Trappists
where I made jelly, sewed chasubles, fed fat chewing sheep,
chanted under a holy nave many a "*Te Deum*"

before a blessed cross under a mere pin-light
that perfumed my heart with an insight into a heavenly world
that proved electricity real. I learned to pray!

I felt as I looked at the holy men around me
too inferior to feel anything close to saintly, God forbid.
Suretyship for sure was the precursor of ruin,

although humility, to me, always bore a taint
of inhuman artificiality, and whenever I sought to give it
attentive patience I abhorred the meekness

in myself it demanded of otherworldliness,
for to me the gateway to win the respect and favor of God
was *being real*, clearly the ultimate grace.

Had I adequate faith? For St. Augustine
the recovered self is in all matters, a renewed, transcended self
which explains how that man could recall

his abject sinning self without sinning again
by his working memory. I worked diligently to seine the past
for some continuity to some future, shining.

The unfathomable deep longing of the soul
is surely rabid to vex itself, to offer violence to its own nature,
impelling it to its own muddled prosecution

to take its final lesson in the iron-clasped
volume of despair. "Ah, starry hope that didst rise
but to be overcast!" I had read my Poe.

Was I any worse than the confused St. Paul
of Romans 7:15-25 whose vocalizations I decoded as working
against myself: "I do not understand what I do.

For what I want to do, I do not do, but what I hate
I do." Yes! "And if I do what I do not want to do, I agree the law
is good. As it is, it is no longer I myself who do it,

but it is sin living in me. For I do not do the good
I want to do, but the evil I do not want to do—this I keep on doing.
Now if I do what I do not want to do, it is no longer

I who do it, but it is sin living in me that does it."
Talk of waging war against the law of the mind! Jabberwocky
it may be to average men, yet it spoke directly to me!

I cared that my Lord Jesus carried his cross for me,
the black *weight* of the thing, aware that no one ever mentions
in prayer—or thinks of—His *shoulder* wounds!

A flowing river cut through every duplicity in life
that promised Lord Jesus's endless substitutionary love for me,
a faith I have never once lost or relinquished,

but inevitably, I was a recusant, defiant,
bold, objecting to any other authority and its mutt-like face,
a smug and credulous Papist unbudgeable,

as deaf as Goya, hating the word *fellowship*,
sitting up in the craggy mountains of my own puffed-up being,
no joy seeds planted within my heart-soil.

No need in me was as close to or as deep
as my dark nightmares, making me the bed wetter that I was
who avoided waking up to treacherous reality,

diving into the lower depths of sleep, fleeing
what lay await for me awake, accusations of me being me.
So many of the peculiar mysteries that I ran to

were explained by the mystifications I ran from,
my fears becoming a kleptopredator who stole my mind
and then proceeded to devour me, as well.

I regarded any praise as unsaid, inconfident
of my true place in life, my mind a big neep of hesitations
my wishes tall but rare as fields of blewits.

Didn't Leonardo illustrate for us that man could
fit inside a square and a circle both? I myself searched to find
then where I myself might connect, attach, unite.

Was it so haughty of me, so vain, to need
to interpret my own life as other than a formulated creature,
the projected product of some worthy syndrome,

lest in my own charmless but hopeful eyes
I become objectionable to the very me parading the black halls
my awkward pedestrian self perambulated?

Scarecrows with heads carved out of mangel-wurzels
and stuffed with sawdust constituted the barking wastrels who ran
with me. I *looked* in part like Worzel Gummidge,

had his sulks, disappeared like him, but also in part
resembled Henry Wriothesley (rhymes with wisely!) Shakespeare's
bosom friend—wasn't he the "fair youth" of the sonnets—

and bore his pulled nose but assure you I was no Adonis!
Cock of the rooks, effigy, bird-scarer, I would dress in black to look
like the 16th-century poet whose name I mimed for laughs.

I wrote dramas, giving players my own opinions
full of pages with climaxes that were long and more drawn-out
than Wagner's ending to the overture to *Rienzi*,

truths not found in me because they were useful,
but found because it was possible to find them! I loved words
and the wild, impish, somersaulting tumbles

they could perform, sought to write pages to be loved,
preaching through personae, rare, odd, multi-voiced puppetry
in funny masks that grinned and groaned

through whatever dreamt-up infamy narratives
that might outlast me lest love be locked out. So, was I too odd
to succeed on this scary irrational planet of ours?

Couldn't others see that I had an electric mind,
nearly photographic recall, selves to share? In dreams I anticipated
pending, peopled perspectives of development.

I can say I was *hurt* by life into poetry and crossed
the Clopton Bridge from Medford into my own mysterious London,
the role of looker-on foreordained by fate,

although my hectic scribblings, while never born
of a disinterested rubric, were nothing whatsoever compared to
the acrimonious ravings of my inner mind, but

God-fearing, the rind of one apple tasted true.
"Hang there like fruit, until the tree must die!" I cried to myself,
calling from the tincture of my lurid face.

I could turn a free, obliging hand to any poem
with luxuriant ease and soon dreamt I was a scop in Heorot,
that wondrous hall, singing of God's creation.

I chased my rude and raw red visions
like the Hebrew prophets did their own (or so I thought)
when the spirit of God took me by the hair,

and I felt exiled, baggage on my shoulder,
my face masked, as I dug through a deep hole like Ezekiel
only to observe through my writing no world

but odd, creeping things, abominable beasts,
and idols, fetishes, drawn upon the walls of rooms, more
than seventy selves worshipping my art.

It was as if I had a sudden reflection of myself,
pursuing fame, stumbling over the need only to discover
the face I hoped to be heroic had proved vile.

Was Marx correct when he said of legal institutions
they could not stand higher than the society that brought the forth?
I admit I've always been a famous version of myself,

with a word to the fates not to be a symptom
of the times I wished to transform. I saw I was a law unto myself,
not above nor below, only beyond my peers.

Who cared what kind of shirt or shouting slogan
the murdering party wears, whether it is attacking working slobs
or in-bred toffee-nosed silver spoon wankers.

Life, or so I saw, left me a witless anthropophobe,
Still, I insisted I be saved even if through those sins and sorrows
I abjured in and by a pious, desperate repentance,

to be worthy of the benevolent God that made me
and my face and my vagrant need to expend my talent and tact.
I badly, very badly, had to *matter* in my mind.

I cherished my intuition, which Einstein declared
was the only truly valuable thing to have, considering my brain
a limited frontier with defined, restricted borders.

That I was me made me what I was, for merely
being different now mattered to me. There are Goshens everywhere,
same name, same state, same nation.

What did the Jumblies keep in a sieve? *Afloat*
is the answer, a simple one. But surely buoyancy was nothing
at all to boast about, except I did not sink.

"*Non fui, fui, non sum non curio.*" So read
a cool Epicurean gravestone of the ancient Roman empire,
but that was not my epitaph, not even close.

Wash myself with water as I might, laving,
Almighty God's plan allows for the irrational, the discordant,
the odd, the inexplicable. What is bald obedience

worth without knowledge? Adam scarfed
the forbidden fruit and spat out me, my face, my name, my voice,
unimprovably all that I had to give.

Yet I needed to *signify*, not mimic brainless
fresh snow absorbing sound, lowering ambient noise over lands
I traversed. Non-persons unperson persons, see?

Anonymity is a desperate kind of failure
is not a saint's remark, and yet, although I felt ashamed, guilty
of my reach, my aspirations, ambition bit me,

for as Pelagius declared, "If I ought, I can."
Ought *implies* can! The free will we have that he preached
filled me with a bleak and terrible resolve

to march, an alien, through the Forest of Arden,
although I felt far, far stranger there than ever I did at home.
But then travelers must look about content,

and if I felt somewhat homesick for my real self
when among the unappetizing mask-wearers and meat puppets
who well succeeded in this farcical world,

life among those fat, greedy ruin-bibbers
who seem never, never friends of Jesus or his Holy Cross,
being as sadly secular as they seem to be,

I prayed to re-create what God created
and tried to be free as the Purple Martin and its sounding song
of boisterous, throaty chirps and creaky rattles.

I worked in seclusion and built my poems
like a Hadrami his mud-brick tower, futuristic but peculiar
constructions that were as foolish as forfeit

and that no one read. I tried like a fool to cloak
my incompetence, to impersonate what denied my hollowness
the way wooers of the world consistently do.

I came to see how language was a lexicon
of emancipation to help one make sense of life's complexities,
the beginning of which St. John assured us.

Begotten, not made! The infinite *power* of Jesus
Who might sit on my pen! Generated by procreation, it means
in the creed—fathered forth! Wasn't to beget

to create? *Crescere!* To arise, be born, increase,
grow, very like God restoring the hot radiance of his own glory
shining through his Son and in and through us!

I determined that, since belief was the engine
that made perception operate, how, by actively disguising
my own unhappiness, I could remedy it.

"Play the man," Master Ridley," said Hugh Latimer
about to be burned at the stake at Oxford in 1555. Or better
was it to "Play the man I am," as said Coriolanus,

recoiling at the outrage of having to act a part,
complete with frilly costume, dialogue, and stage directions,
that did not correspond with his inner truth?

If you want something that you have never had,
you must be willing to do something you never have done, no?
Shape a *persona*, moron, I told myself—and be it!

That there is no description of Jesus Christ
in the whole of the New Testament bade me feel I myself
may shape-shift a fit semblance—why not?—

transcending the grim, impossible illusion
that I had to be what, when looking down at me as bloatware,
onlookers surmised I would be nothing else.

I prayed to be the lacerated shoulder that no one
mentions of Christ's pain, the beaten flesh and laid-bare bones
inflicted upon him, that somehow I might

if nothing else, although deeply unworthy,
stand for something that no one in this dim world ever notices?
Might that not be my legacy? But all along I thought

don whatever mask you will, be no fanfaroon
to falsify the basic you! Spring travels about the same rate
as a parent pushing a stroller, and I begged

my fate not unnaturally bumrush the weather
that composed the scenery of my life. I wanted to be loyal
to God's ideal nature and, so, be true to my own.

Let no tide, neap or spring, ever drown me.
John Wesley's rule was always to look a mad mob in the face,
and as I tried to configure my metaphysics

thumbfumbled from one dumb job to another,
a high school stationery clerk, a sand hog, a fledgling linotypist
with inky face and black hands holding slugs.

I sought identity as being, not becoming,
not jiggling pocket change in a doorway like some scarlet pimp,
nor wasting away my life like some silly *fandangero*.

I was a born antinomian, secretly despised
restraints and rules but feared much and, like the Arabian horse,
hated a slap or a blow, regarding most insults

and other's opinions as left unsaid, mentally
tricing them up in the rigging and taking Fate's I-felt-deserved
hot bitter lashes, but I always walked away.

I was a criminal bed-wetter. Imagination
became my only reality, and I drove hard into sleep for refuge,
refusing to awake for any reason at all,

avoiding the scary ongoing parade of hideous facts
that daily waited to confront me whenever I awoke. Plunging
to the depths whales swam into, the dark benthic,

became my sole salvation until I would wake
sopping wet, high tide and low, only to learn again the secret
to art is like an intrepid sailor going too far.

Some Samarkand always lay over the horizon
for me in my dreams, but feeling deep down in my heart
that any compensating equivalence would do.

I began to mill about with the local precariat,
watching fools ambush-market their mediocrity to the world,
bowing belly low and scraping. And me?

I had a pen and began to push it across pages
from the mounting piles of screed at my elbow that scorned
my incompetence in scowling back at me.

I confess I fell in love any number of times
with worthy girls and also with some witches, trulls and tarts,
trying to cope with the confounding paradox

that, while I had to be in love in order to create,
I discovered that being in love only weakened my efforts,
realizing through various relationships, good

and bad, that the banal that you would interpret
is more mysterious than any of its opposites, its weird truths
to be had only by a transfiguring imagination,

which I had in abundance, along with visions
as sharp as my pencils and pens, not a one as disloyal
as the women I very soon felt happier without.

Art was my salvation to try to remake what I
in the world inherited, whether hare-drummer, Fritz, gnome,
cavalier, Mouse King, or Nutcracker soldier.

I deeply prayed that I might signify enough
to make part of heaven weep for me and my blunders—to count
myself justified, even if by way of God's pity,

believing that if I pulled hard enough on midnight
I could unroll the dawn and find in daybreak a sunrise bright
enough to galvanize my heart with electricity!

"Give me neither poverty (lest I resent you)
or riches (lest I forget you)"—St. Augustine's gentle prayer—
was basically my own feeble one, except that

I pled—I begged—only not to be a donkeystone.
Augustine declared, "Love means: I want you to be!" I was—
or, I swear, at least I so pretended to be—

so, may I ask, that gets me nothing, I who swore
I need not have been a soldier in full-parade uniform, nutcracker
    cute,
who expected no Clara or Marie to buss my bum?

Moses pervertedly killed a man, and so did David,
and the good Godfather, reaching into his grab-bag of dolls and
    dollars,
allowed them solid profiles the world adored,

so, why let the poor Gringoire that I am, I asked,
be a dry ball of failure? I will play any role you offer, Councilor
    Grand,
please, *please*, let me only be a nut that cracks!

Horton's Radishes

"Nobody cannot grow radishes" is an old saw.
But Horton Pineweevil with his Burpee seeds
found bright red interiors beneath white skin
when they poked through the ground in August.

The tangerine-sizes seemed all damn wrong!
Were these *watermelons*, green-shouldered,
idiotically scarlet, supposed to be flavorful,
unlike real radishes, which are *white* within?

"You a New Hampshire screwdriver!" barked
his old man, flat-slapping down his bird-bill hat.
"Planting seeds when acorns line the walkways?
A brown fog out so thick you can hardly spit?"

Horton had read to plant the seeds in winter,
which he did in his small patch in Brunswick,
following the tiny directions on the envelope,
but, like most Pineweevils, he was a failure,

or so his father snapped. "You a mudboy,
Hort, always wuz. Dumb as a box of hair!
No lamps burning and two ships at sea, fer
*chris*ssakes! What do you repre*sent*, mutt,

a flower-pot judge? Wouldn't know beans
if the goddam bag were untied! *Look at me!*
All the windows frozen?" Nobody had told him
they were *Chinese* radishes, good for putting up,

as most working Down East housewives know
come pickling time, boiling them up with salt,
vinegar, garlic, if they'd not good bulbs handy.
Horton, gnawing his fingernails, felt despair.

"Don't make knee-odds to me what you do,"
grizzled his father, sniting snot to the side,
"save that folks talk, dammit, don't you see,
so, it's *me* to explain you bein' brain dead!

Mrs. Delicato wanted you for an errand boy
two summers back, 'til you went and backed
into her fence-gate toting a bag of groceries
and sprung the goddam lock open. *And why?*

To time save! Not looking! Lazy man's load!
Heedless as a dicksissel! Being fast asleep
at the switch don't do it, boy, OK? Your head
is up your fat ass so far you can't pull it out!"

I used to see Horton, looking lost, in Big Yank
Jeans at yard sales in Topsham and Wiscasset,
examining old field tools, thumb-rubbing them,
while his father sat glumly in their old De Soto,

growing red and angry, blasting the car horn,
when Horton would go pale, drop the items,
and make for the car with resigned gestures
to his father about things he wanted to grow.

West Barnstable Cemetery

I gently stroll our two babies along the tiny paths
where hoary graves prove the reality of mortality,

with many stones filled with nominal exhortations,
Makepeace, *Lovegood*, *Hopewell*, and *Goodspeed*,

19th-century markers looming like bitten lozenges,
granite gray, some with frills, entablature designs

favoring dado or wainscoting at the bottom, a field
in the middle maybe, a frieze or cornice at the top.

Breedloves are there, but you will find no *Bonifaces*,
no foreign names, no peculiar graves, no *Eye*-talians,

for example, can be seen buried under little hillocks,
excavated, reserved solely for tut-mouthed Yankees.

These were the venerable old families, worthy tombs,
sepulchers, old vaults, burial chambers, mausoleums,

chipped dark stone crypts that one might call fancy.
Older gravesites, the final resting place of puritans,

sea captains, thin, bearded men who wore timepieces
depending from their vests, readers of hard Scripture

and flinty with rectitude, are 300 or more years buried,
lying with their wives and daughters named *Constant*,

Tamsun, Knought, Zilpah, Aquila, Rebekah, Lately,
Pelatah, Deliverance, Phipenny, Piety, Experience,

Temperance, Handmade, Obedience, Forsaken, Dust,
Credence, Thankful, and *What-God-Will,* each serving

as well, as lessons to us as superstitiously we roll past
along with pious exhortations—*Repent, Remember,*

Submit, Patience, Silence, Giveway, and *Prudence.*
I believe I also saw a *Humiliation.* I'll confess I was

in the beginning unprepared, even shocked, to read,
to *hear,* the bull-trumpeting echoes of the Last Days

of 2 Timothy 3, when miscreants like me, fools of folly,
lovers of their own selves, proud covetous boasters,

rude blasphemers, lapsers disobedient to parents, and
unholy, shall reap the gusts of oncoming whirlwinds,

and as if proof of it we all three soon failed to heed
reproaches, me and our fallen babies, weak sinners—

or was it that the exhorting names seemed dull clichés?—
and, worse, wheeling past the frowning graves, I sang

softly. Still, pushing the pram, I felt far too God-fearing
(and spooked!) not to follow the straight cemetery paths,

not for a minute, as we rolled toward the stonewall exit,
pausing even to *consider*—ever—taking any shortcuts!

Richard M. Nixon

> "The man whom Truman had detested personally more than any other figure with whom he ever came in contact . . . the man who in 1952 called Truman a traitor . . . the man whom Truman used to call 'squirrelhead,' not merely privately but also on one public occasion."
> —Robert H. Ferrell, *Dear Bess*

A king is created by others, can be played
by any actor who's a mediocrity, nobody exceptional.
Well-played subjects can turn a shadow

on stage into a monarch through certain
behavior toward him alone. Power is a phenomenon
connivingly created by group dynamics,

never solely by the "powerful man."
It calls, creates, him into being. A king is forged by
—and in—the flashing fire of others.

In secret, the king seeks to find a foothold
in the slippery network of lackeys validating him.
A king is always played by others.

See that tall boob in the repertory? Hand
him that corona, and, by mere puppetry and blocking,
stand back to let him merely ventriloquate.

There you have your yakking projection,
O, in any ermine you sling around his waiting neck
—now just kowtow toward your selection.

Whither Went the Lad I Once Knew?

Whither went the lad I once knew?
Why did he run away?
Did he break free in a mood of rue
and leave with nothing to say?

Had he the view of the man he'd be,
insufferable to his gaze?
Was his foresight of envisioning me
blight to his playful days?

Was the reason for saying goodbye
the refusal to be as I am,
an empty suit even I can't descry
a groping, untidy old man?

A Goodbye to a Baby's a Great Betrayal

A goodbye to a baby's a great betrayal,
a modulated hug, a varied, false portrayal.
You knife their dreams by walking away.
To that stranger caressing her, he is prey.

Perfidy projects in mists a missing father,
instantly unpersons any real figure, rather
like falling through an avoirdupois of air
or some prankster snatching back a chair.

Leaving her with a noise of an iron wheel
is as merciless and cruel as trying to steal
away with a reechy kiss of a Judas thief,
fracturing equally any bond or true belief.

Just a hint of any trickery erodes support.
A letdown floods a memory, can abort
scads of love, and skewer all perception,
creating an orphan *and* lifelong deception.

Why Sail to the Limberlost?

Why sail to the Limberlost? What's the place to me?
    Some strange necromancy
    Made charming by a fancy
That no part of my life claims for the spot as its key.

When can any Arcadia fashioned by some pluming pen,
    Born of fevered brow
    Teach my poor soul how
The world I see around me is never a monstrous fen?

How is the essence of joy the nature of picturesque
    As gaseous as vapor
    Attenuated as paper
While I inhabit a globe from which I'm dispossessed?

Where is human affection not fenced by bitter thorn,
    Anxious to publicize
    Tricks by way of eyes
Bidding me full welcome but showing me only scorn,

What sunlight may do to entertain let others mark,
    A bridge across their weir
    While turning a deaf ear
I prefer to attend to my death here in the utter dark.

When Wee Shenandoah Bites and Chews a Popsicle

When wee Shenandoah bites and chews a Popsicle
what can be heard are crunches in her perfect head,
as much a prayer as vibrations, a muffled grinding

sound, *munch, chomp, crunch,* much reverberating
in her face, a gingersnap of sheer delight. I notice
she attends to little else while snapping at her ice,

enchanted, staring blankly into the middle distance,
a manducating attention usurping itself in the way
a dream is consumed. Her hands employ the stick,

re-twisting it, in musical accompaniment, for song
is part of all she nibbles and gnaws, and, like prayer,
seeks in the very act a human plea for perfect joy.

No One's Happier Than When He Holds a Handful of Flamingo

No one is happier than when holding a handful of flamingo,
pink in the wildness of its fluff. It yips to return your delight,

caught up by any human's love, preferring to any rising flight
the warmth of a loving man with no birdlike community jingo.

Its pink feathers as they swell rise to perfuse your happy hand,
filling both your soul, and its, with the height of highest pingo,

as both gay bird and man consciously meet in a matching bingo
where for one moment no one, ecstatic, makes a single demand.

Mickey Mouse's Mug
a sonnet

First, he has no eyebrows, the glaring sign of a geek,
a lower lip like Mel Tormé's but decidedly no upper,
then strangely for a rodent he sports a widow's peak
as pointedly sharp and black as any horse's crupper.
A mouse's ears are small but not so Mickey Mouse's,
sursealed, physiologically, from any act of listening;
so, what explains big oval discs—to keep out louses?
His nose is comically a bulb, pert, round, glistening,
despite the glaring fact most mice's snouts are pointed.
There is no chin, to speak of, both eyes pop like corn,
while his wobbling limbs belie a notion he is jointed,
and when he's talking the vocal sound's 9/10th horn!
Who's the leader of the club that's made for you and me?
I would say any mouse remotely real—*with no anomaly!*

Rhubarb Has a Voice

Rhubarb has a voice. Its saturated cells crackle in the dark.
The docile plants are moved to pitch-black "forcing sheds"

after two long years in the fields. Being dumb, rubes think
they can *feel* underground and so spend their stored-up root-

energy by growing taller at a ridiculous rate. They rebound
and snap; if you are quiet in the sheds, their red mutterings,

rose red, can be *heard* and reach up, toward savage sunlight
that they will not and never see again: rebarbatively think,

striving to reboot, re-resuming boldly, bending like a boom.
A barbarous plant, damaged by hard *cold*, cannot be eaten,

as it may be high in oxalic acid, migrating from the leaves
and, so, cause illness, rebelliously, rebuking you like guilt,

but in sheds it's loamy warm, replenishing by somber dark
what in a small conversation will any conversation sweeten

and, just by speaking, its crackle, by way of secret cackle,
like any rubious, docile, dumbness, soon rebound rebuilt!

So Dear to My Heart Made Life Unreal for Me

Nothing in life ever lived up to the rustic paradise so braided to my heart
and soul—I still recall every scene—as that endearing Walt Disney film,

with its woods, open meadows, animals, horses, hot golden sun, cornstalks;
when Burl Ives crooned, "Lavender Blue," as happily as ol' Uncle Remus

brightly sang "Zip-a-Dee-Doo-Dah" in *Song of the South,* I melted with love.
It opened with a fairy book, panning in on rotogravures of holiday memories.

I was only eight and watched it with Aunt Gert in Boston at the Paramount,
my hands warm in my lap, the majestic nave above, its angels and trumpets

blowing as the purple curtain swung open wide, when sudden darkness fell,
plaiting mystery to an enchantment I'd never known, twisting into two plies

my small heart and no end of flexible Technicolor dreams that gave cordage
to no reality I ever saw again, not once in real life, never in the waking world.

As I watched handsome Bobby Driscoll in his sailor suit and collar
or blouse
and pretty Luana Patten as "Tidy" in a pink dress, capering black
lambs, cows,

dirt roads, fireplaces, butterflies, chipmunks, bare feet, bouncing
rabbits,
trains, split-rail fences, flowers, Granny, General Jackson pulling a
plow,

Jeremiah Kincaid was tied to my soul, as were sweet Johnny and
Ginny.
Nothing indicated that poor young Driscoll would be found dead at
thirty-one,

lying on a cot with empty beer bottles and religious pamphlets on
the floor.
The New York medical examiner determined he had died from
heart failure

caused by a severe case of hardening of the arteries due to longtime
drug abuse.
No identification was found on the body. Photos shown around the
neighborhood

yielded no positive identification. His body went unclaimed, and he
was buried
in an unmarked pauper's grave in New York City's Potter Field on
Hart Island.

If true generosity towards the future lies in giving all to the present,
as Camus says,
sever me, detach me, disconnect me, separate me, disassociate me
from this day on.

Hosta Blue Cadet as a Civil War Memorial

There is in this misty blue wedded to gray
what once summoned armies in battle array.

A touch of care in its heart-shaped leaves
recalls in memory how a country grieves

in pleading God's mercy for no end of dead,
slain in their youth with their prayers unsaid.

Its mounding habit like sad drumlin graves,
dotting bowed hillsides in unbroken waves,

proves by symbol, the way that colors merge,
that a century's hostilities effectively purge

the way foes come to see that prayer may grant
divine grace for both in this small border plant.

All Crows Are Sentries

All crows are sentries,
always on duty, forever at war. They can count
up to six, know the smell

of gunpowder, thrive in worrying
foxes into giving up their dinners, cultivate purple voices,
know the sides of a hemlock tree,

and perpetually fold their wings
precisely three times after perkily alighting, fastidiously,
to be certain it is neatly done.

Being mistaken for common evil
in the blackness has taught them well that world evil
comes mainly from ignorance.

A horned owl terrifies a crow.
As Albert Camus has told us, an intellectual is someone
whose waking mind watches itself,

and both sets of knowing birds
who do not create experience but have undergone it,
can easily fancy themselves caught,

therefore, catch themselves first
by beaky vigilance, fighting never to forget stupidity
has a knack of getting its own way.

Real Estate Advisors

President Dick Nixon admired swarthy "Bebe" Rebozo,
—both loved charbroiled steaks and show tunes—who bought him
places in Key Biscayne and worked as his private james.

Nixon also hustled Bob Abplanalp, owner of Grand Cay
in the Bahamas, who invented the aerosol valve and so bought him
his thirty-acre ranch in San Clemente (without any quitclaims).

Thus, Bebe and Bobby showed their immigrant servitude
and in exchange for serving his whims—for billions they bought him
—Dick impressed wheedlers by stoking their paltry aims.

So, these three hucksters swapped their ambitions with joy,
two rabid Republicans happily bumsucked Nixon and bought him,
and yet, to the end, *he could never pronounce their names.*

Dim Bulb

for E.T.

"Hugh Kingsmill believed that life
was divided, not between men and
women, Tory and Labor, or even one
nationality or another, but between
people of will and of imagination."
—*Manchester Guardian*

As Galileo was given to see
by fat Jupiter's moons that Earth revolves
while never standing still,

it was by an opposite decree
you revealed how valued trust dissolves
by a cold and unbudging will.

Henry Thoreau in His Garret at 225 Main St. Concord, Mass.

As full truth of
what Jesus said

needs a lifetime
study being read,

lyrics outlast
singing of song.

Life is short,
and Art is long.

At Walden Henry
with keen intent

living dutifully
two years spent.

Longer by far as
he spent living it,

he spent twelve years
by pencil giving it

in a narrow room,
and a journal, too,

with Min, his cat,
a window view,

green pine desk,
driftwood chair,

pages compiled,
the solitary heir

for us to read
of one endeavor,

explaining nature
goes on forever.

Poet and Peasant Overture

In high Peru, the original home of potatoes
which peasants crave as much as tomatoes,

they hoe them by hand wearing hats of reds
fast on their heads as they scumble the beds,

turning over leaves, buds, fruits, and seeds,
proving a vegetable love fills Lima's needs.

Potato heads, hats of red, brown rows hoed
reveal manner is means and means a mode.

Catbriar

Vines are commonly ropy but these are never soft, their tentacles
harder looping than the fashion of bracelets women tempt you by,

swirling in beguiling spin. These are close bitten, of no gender
but neutered in the rude way eunuchs are docked, raising in ire

teeth, claws, nails, spikes, thorns all working to tear your face,
piercing you like teeth that will not let you go just walking by.

No satanic goatsnake outbites catbriar with its leg-ripping thorns,
snagging you in arrowsharp evil even when cut, theoretically dead.

It *snaps* at you, bitchily hitches your pants as you try to walk away,
climbing tenaciously over itself, bitter at being smugly held a shrub.

Greenbrier, bullbrier, horsebrier are other diabolical aliases it likes,
refusing even to go under the same name, another of its deviances.

A bold octopus boiled by spit and trimmed by savage hail and heat,
it corrodes the concept that vines rise with nature in any holy sense.

Does the vine point to Eve's troublesome dream, and did her hair
prefigure like Eden's unpruned foliage how cats so easily ensnare?

Shiloh and Shenny's Seawater Green Eyes

"I pity the man who doesn't have daughters."
—Karl Marx

Shiloh and Shenny's seawater green eyes
enlighten my life in the way of surmise,

glowing brightly electric in merry vaunt,
commanding yet another story they want.

It is through such incandescent windows
one need merely look for saving rainbows

to bring me joy in those days when I fail,
when my probing mind proves to be frail,

restoring my hope by their innocent sight,
four little eyes gleaming Christmas bright.

Hats

As a plant with a seed on its head
distinctly has plans in its verdant mind, thanks
to nature, to go walking at once,

whoever dully sits has a cone instead,
which equally reveals its sloth, eyes like blanks,
with the pointed head of a dunce.

"Holiday for Strings"

"The most appreciative listeners are always those who know nothing about music."
—David Rose

Andre Kostelanetz, Morton Gould.
Not classical, not pop
But somewhere in the middle,
Strings over brass.
Life is far too short,
Give them a pass.

Skitch Henderson, Billy Rose.
Little rhythm, mostly glop
Hear the tell-tale fiddle?
Incompetently crass.
You are given one life,
Waste it not on gas.

Henry Mancini, Miklos Rozsa.
Vaporous meanderings
Unmemorable sheer piddle
With nothing of class
Choose gold in this life,
Not tinkling brass.

John Williams, Maurice Jarre.
Any loon was better.
Naught but noisy diddle,
Transparent as glass.
Be original in life.
Never go *en masse*.

Mitchell Ayres, Frank Chacksfield, Leroy Anderson.
Musical clichés
Not so much as a riddle.
Strictly string bass.
Travel straight in life.
Allow no impasse.

Victor Young, Peter Nero. Michel Legrand.
Cack from the very jump
Any way you twiddle.
Musical crabgrass.
Fall in love with beauty
Not into a crevasse.

Percy Faith, Bert Kaempfert, Ray Coniff.
The pain, the pain.
At best pure taradiddle.
Nothing was more crass.
Quality in music
Rarely showed less class.

Herb Alpert, Mantovani, Burt Bachrach.
Search for words
Lower than second fiddle!
How about morass?
Which perfectly describes
A quagmire of gaseous mass.

Roger Williams, Les Baxter, Lawrence Welk.
Imperscrutable kitsch.
Noise with a little tiddle.
Best played in a crevasse
Cheap, gimcrack, tawdry,
Beware, any who trespass.

Joshua Tree

Mormon pioneers fully believed they were waving,
like the Old Testament prophets, beckoning us to the promised land,
with gnarled craving hand, teeth like daggers,

their ill-smelling fruit a cluster of nubbly pods,
whose sticky pollen cannot be carried by wind, only by yucca moth
which fertilizes the flower and then lays eggs

in the ovary. The caterpillars hatch by the time
seeds are developed and munch them, leaving enough to guarantee
the species. Bitter, acrid, sour, and useless,

the fruit was historically used as a laxative or
to prevent lice infestations, its harsh wood making a good knife blade
or spindle on cotton wood to whip up a fire

to help that perennial shrub called Man
just as dagger-hearted, teeth cruel, rasping, misshapen, and pleading,
seedy, bitter, and quite as often useless,

green, yellow, bent, and aged, a poor dreamless
Giacomettian isolato, juddery, gesturing in the very middle of woeful
insufficiency for anyone at all's succor.

J'Accuse

Most mothers, wittingly or not, want us to see through our fathers,
working by wiles and guile to win by sin the lifelong parent battle,
trying as best they can to blame them for all complaints and bothers
so, to fulfill by a hideous fiat of fate their preternatural gift to tattle,

but then how explain the failure of these talent-evaluating bitches
to realize that in their sweeping generalizations and shifting blame
brooming is the first and foremost sign and symbol of all witches
and that accusing in almost every instance is the *accuser's* shame?

Asthma

I hear in my wheezes the colloquies
of loons, strident as the high whistles of the Santa Fe
blowing south. Are they within me,

resonances weirdly fluting just at dusk,
wails to frighten anyone, *whooooing*, long, mournful,
like one red-eye answering another,

evoking mystery, punctuating the fall
 of night, part of me wrapped up in that vocalization?
Solitude often makes my lake-sounds

moan like a ghost in a tree summoning
myself over wind, as if I am ready to devour vertebrate
prey headfirst, like loons digestible fish

nor does my pointy bill hesitate to stab
or grasp prey when I see them visible through the water
as if the very source of my wheezes.

Shiloh and Shenandoah Walking at 20 Months

Shiloh's long, loping, clump-footed stride,
—*thump, thump*, she proceeds on her heels—
reflects in its uniqueness a strident pride.

Shenny rolls like a mariner just off a ship,
crossing a room the way a bunny steals,
flirting the while with a shake of her hip.

Wayfarers, both, show the curious knack
of Mr. Lincoln who declared of his streels,
"I'm a slow walker but I never walk back."

Threnody from a Child

I look in great fear toward the purple dark.
My thin arms lay white, with the window stark,
the roof above flattened by walking wind.

Are the fields now wet where the locusts grow,
where thorns claw birds as the wild winds blow,
reminding me in my bed that I have sinned?

A blue mist creeps toward the bedroom walls,
my limp hair lay thin from the governess brush,
motion leaves frightened from my quiet hands
as if doom hastens inward with a terrible rush.

§

I look with some fear toward the purple dark.
My thin arms lay white, with the window stark,
the roof above flattened by walking wind.

Are the forests waving in some midnight fear,
as leaves from the witching sky snatch and tear,
waking to tell me that the world has dimmed?

A blue mist creeps toward my bedroom walls,
my limp hair lay thin from the governess brush,
motion leaves frightened from my quiet hands
as if doom hastens inward with a terrible rush.

Flashback

Of all
the darknesses
from the
somber specters of night
that
upon reflection
I see

the worst
is the
ungodly killing memory
of my father saying
"You were never right"
looking directly
at me.

The Day Augustus Saint-Gaudens Introduced Robert Louis Stevenson to General William Tecumseh in the Palace Hotel

"Was he one of my boys?" asked old General Sherman.
"No, no," said Gus, "he is the illustrious novelist from Scotland,
the fellow who wrote *Dr. Jekyll and Mr. Hyde*."

"Well, he's no fool. Let him come up," muttered
the slightly dotty general, lying prone on a sofa. Once, they so met,
three geniuses who convened in a single room.

The young master sculptor had been working hard
on what now stands the Sherman Memorial, at the Southeast Corner
of Central Park, and thrilled at the chance to see

two polymaths together, he whose $20 gold piece—
with, on one side, a wind-swept Liberty striding forward, her gown
billowing in the wind, lit by the rays of a rising sun,

and on the other an eagle in flight—is still considered
to be the most beautiful coin ever created. (He never lived to see
it minted, dying in 1907, before the coin was struck.

An enthusiastic Sherman then garrulously explained
to Mrs. Fanny Stevenson the serious difference between saber-cuts
("They made you look done up, without doing harm")

and bullet wounds ("They zip right though you,"
he squawked and poked Fanny in the middle of her tummy).
They looked at maps, which the thin Scot admired,

as he knew many of the battles of the Civil War.
Gus who had been the catalyst of this historic meeting was truly
worshipped by both men, having memorialized

both in art, designing a low-relief portrait of Louis,
surely a gem, as well as the great masterpiece of the Union
General. What a trinity! Sculptor, writer, soldier!

Sherman sculpted out many battles in Georgia.
Saint-Gaudens fought battles in bronze. While Stevenson wrote
like a recording angel, greeting a planet's dawns.

"Deep Throat"

> "It had nothing to do with patriotism. It was spite."
>
> —Alexander Theroux

Mark Felt, FBI number two, hated Nixon
for passing him over as director in favor
of an outsider, Patrick Gray, so to fix him,
retaliated (covertly), his revenge to savor.

Abstract Expressionist Paintings Are Spat Out

> "But I found a lot of the artists at the Cedar Bar were difficult for me to talk to. It almost seems that there were many more of them sharing some common idea than there was of me."
> —Robert Rauschenberg

Abstract Expressionist paintings are spat out. Their images are
 queer.
Who believes the difficult problems of consciousness can be resolved

by humans? Only fools with dead nerves in their eyelids hope for
 such.
I count myself among the Mysterians with bulbous question-mark
 heads,

among the simple fideists heeding St. Paul, who teaches faith holds
 sway.
Modern museum walls are strictly comic, replete with framed
 abortions.

Jasper Johns, Robert Rauschenberg, Ellsworth Kelly, James
 Rosenquist,
left us only the cantos of sodomites, campy variations of balls and
 penises,

gestural gay imagery, stark, profane, all drowning in lunatic
 homoerotica.
Agnes Martin's insane grids are basically tantrums, nose-thumbing
 spats—

dense, minute striations of rote pencil lines with odd primary color
    washes
of diluted acrylic paints, delineated graphite grids that speak of
    imbecility.

All Ab Ex art madly strove to stand in for speech, making frazzled
    attempts
to articulate self-presence before a void. One but sees the work of
    bantams,

lavendrical inarticulates who couldn't draw a cat, using martial
    metaphors
to describe the act of painting, wistfully fobbing off shapes and
    shadows

for words they did not embody like engagement, struggle, victory,
    defeat.
Closeted men were long enjoined from painting as an act of self-
    revelation,

But even if they could paint such revealing pictures, schooled
    brilliance,
how could they ever believe that the images generated by a
    homosexual

could have universal intelligibility? Discernible punch? True artistic
    value?
Gay men, from ages past, never had the luxury of believing in
    expression

as an individual struggle of their weak wills. The art of code
 supplanted that.
Hisses, snaps, spats, *snits* came to define the hubbub of their
 painterly lives.

The unresolvable problem for us is how explain the existence of
 qualia,
individual instances of subjective experience. I understand, I
 understand,

any willing soul with a generous heart must show mercy for
 concepts,
shapes of planar masses, scaled trapezoids, weird triangles positioned

vertically above inverted rhomboids, Rothko swipes, Noland colors,
Reinhardt dribbles, Pollock drips, Olitski drabs, black paintings or
 full white,

even if they prove to be ludicrous geometries and fraudulent color
 compositions;
I merely make the simple plea that such hollow masks, feeble
 executions

in paint as fake as any thespian tricked out in his symmetricals, now
 cease
from lying that such subjective paintings are anything more than an
 excuse.

Oh, Get on With It, for Heaven's Sake! or, the Fault of Films

Each time I go to the movies,
the point has long been made
before scenes end—so dull—

boring me again and again
the bland repetition itself,
making two hours of null.

During that silent film era,
having those titles to *read*?
I'd have gone out of my skull.

Last Request

Bury me please when the sun is out,
not in the cold, cold rain
I want to look down and see myself
safe in this earthly plain
boxed in a warm contain
secure of a final domain
not under a spout in the rain of doubt
where I've been left to drain.

Shenandoah at Two Walks on Her Toes

Shenandoah at two walks on her toes,
as soft as a fairy as on she floats,
pad-pad-padding in midget clothes,
light as a sun slant's tiniest motes.

It is more of a sparkle than a walk,
a toddler's progress of self-delight,
tok-tok-tokking, half cuckoo clock,
half bird ready to spring into flight!

Notice the way that she rows her arms,
the sauciness of that curled lower lip—
her little fanny has its own charms,
along with a cocky spring in her hip.

As I treasure the kiss, her open smile,
the bouncing braid that's Shenny's alone,
I admit as I ponder that rolling style
how her growing up I can try to postpone!

Horseshoe Crab

Any living fossil makes farce of a crumbling Parthenon.
No beast with a mouth between five sets of legs starves.
Book gills are pages, under plates, and dinner is mollusks.
Rigidity in a tail is a way of having a rudder and a baton.
As I squint at its nine eyes, what is it seeing in me, a pole?
Misty sunglow, grim ecru with gamboge, is a kind of music.
I've seen billions in Mispillion Harbor, with giggling eggs.
Females lay between 60,000 and 120,000 eggs in batches.
They mate only on shore, with clanks, hooked in fossil mud.
Swimming upside down, its shape is made for war, assault.
Bait fisheries, yellow as wallpaper, savagery slaughter them.
Their eggs are eaten in places in Southeast Asia and China.
We harvest their blue blood like mad redknots for medicine.
Scientists use it for a fast detection of bacterial endotoxins.
Callow beachgoers kicking desiccated footballs are them.

Herring Gulls

> "[Leopold] Bloom even feeds seagulls,
> which I personally consider nasty birds
> with drunkard's eyes . . ."
> —Vladimir Nabokov, *Lectures on Literature*

The least fussy bird on any list is the herring gull,
part hoover, part cut-rake, part forceps, part scull;

it pries between stones, explores amidst rockweed,
turns over sticks, pecks at blue mud, will overfeed

on anything unlike, say, the choosy Everglade kite,
who will eat apple snails only and nothing else bite.

A gull eats anything: beetles, grasshoppers, clams,
snails, stranded fish, sewage, wiper blades, hams,

compost, popcorn, carrion, women's hats, crickets,
worms, sewage, sand crabs, chubs in the thickets.

They soar high, drop razor clams in order to sup
to crack, split, and with a bang—open them up!

Fresh water is fine as a drink, but seawater works,
for dumping any excess salt is one of their perks.

Their bill is a Swiss Army Knife of proficiency:
a foraging tool—hammer, pliers—of efficiency.

Nothing *is* a "seagull," as such. It is misnamed,
and by mis-appellation is the creature defamed.

Herring gulls overwinter and, rump beside rumps,
all wing south to Manhattan to feast on its dumps,

filled with thousands of acres of garbage and trash
where with hook and tip bills they peck and thrash,

and after every fifteen or so years to one's surprise
their population—predictably—then doubles in size.

Give me for survival neither cockroach nor ant,
neither tardigrades, or yucca, the unkillable plant.

Whom I choose—its body, a-tilt, lifting to sway
—lives riding thermals over warm Cape Cod Bay.

Shiloh's Great Voices

She can voice a full opera at age two and a half;
command like Lord Nelson a complete naval staff

(although they are dolls of all shapes and sizes);
re-interpollate melodies with no end of surprises,

songs from "Kumbaya" to "Be Thou My Vision,"
with an expert organist's calculating precision;

growl like a giant; feign a infant's petulant wail,
providing varying degrees of distress and scale;

mime moods of "very sad," "fearful," and "scared,"
"happy," "shocked," "Oh my goodness," and "weird."

She imitates tolling bells, a toy puppet's thin squeak,
the racing *roarrrrr* of a motorcycle on a blue streak;

How about a knock on the door; bus wiper blades;
a cuckoo clock cuckooing; a car horn when it fades;

the soaring wail of a train on its rumble to Boston?
It's all in the vast repertory that Shiloh's tossed in!

This little tike can emulate any creature's voice
from hedgehog to tree frog, you make the choice,

owl, turkey, peacock, pony, a wolf, Bobbo the ape,
ducks quacking, dogs barking, a bat wearing a cape.

Invention's no problem. She has lyrics to spare,
with ease she snatches them right out of the air.

She sings "Amazing Grace," archaisms included,
with faith in the words (I swear) never excluded;

still when she belts out ABC at the top of her lungs
we hear A-B-C-*B*-E-F-G on those gifted tongues!

A Cat Licking Africa

From a high sky view, as green and brown as brassica,
looking down the dizzy heights soaring high as Aquila,

far beyond the push and pull of any leveling practica,
where immanence shows earthen rocks and lamina,

the shape of Europe, distinctly from a visual maxima,
resembles in scapula and caliber a cat licking Africa.

An Epithalamium for Peter Palandjian and Eliza Dushku, August 18, 2018

A sun-bright future before me set
—I gamble that the shaping fates allow—
for I am by lovely Eliza fervidly beset;
bright shining stars reinforce my vow.
Sing and dance forever in my heart!
Can movie love become a living fact?
O, let my heart forever be the stage
Whenever passion you prefer to act.
Though I exalt your vision seen as duty
like aid for people under foreign skies,
I confess my passion for your beauty
is touched just as grandly by your eyes,
Praise paradox! I bless that I'm undone,
for having lost my heart, I find I've won.

How to Climb a Sand Dune

As the top of a dune moves, with a constant promise of shift,
falling at the windward side, causing it to drift miles in years,

covering anything in its path, including palm trees, villages,
the windward side grows boldly hard and can be walked upon

easily, as can the crest, allowing us to trek, cockily, wockily,
the way we all wish we could slide along wavering tip-tops

of leafy trees, making long giant airy strides like a blue giant.
Always take the scenic route. A top's where one should stand,

where he or she can take the time to look around, sand-rooted,
enfirmed. No dune's a place where another dune does not apply.

If there's one dune, there are ever others. Climbing a soft side
can prove difficult, is best attained by attacking it at an angle.

No Bedouin ever takes his camels up or down a dune, if he
can avoid it. He negotiates the *valleys* between dunes. Jump

off the crest into the slant lee side! If you are lucky, you can
slip-side *alllllllll . . . the . . . waaay . . . to . . . the . . . very . . . bottom!*

Unde de Artesque

The muses are daughters of memory. Memory produces
all the arts, tossing out shadowy, loony notions at night

in the ghostly galleon of one's head. What white moons
cannot rinse out of perfervid hair, flowing open crazily

over any willing and determined skull! Chronochromie is
the color of time, as scintillant a blue as any mysticism is,

to give a willing man of faith his dreaming clouds. When
memories kick in to hasten back into spherical geometry

to re-guess facts, it makes indelible what by recollection
remembrance, reminiscence, you may haunt, revisiting

what non-artists waste for whom openness is a burden,
a corresponding variation of the closed. Mad regions

collapse inward for anyone for whom the many muses
are unwelcome ghosts. Artists race to kiss their breasts!

Suicide in Tenerife

I sought the wood alone where arum lilies grow.
On Orotava in cloudy Tenerife a malignant dwarf
predicted by a pregnant moon I'd come to know
in a dark meeting, a bent crone by a broken wharf.

I took a steep walk up a flight of dark stony stairs.
Ne Cede Arduis ("yield to no obstacle") read a sign.
Stripping off my clothes, I shed equally my cares,
nor did I to that strange exhortation once incline,

when, finding the wood I discovered white lilies
in mad profusion into which I libidinously rolled.
My body imprint formed a ship, my heel Achilles
trust, for I was stabbed by a waiting witch as cold

as the cruel sea crashing on Valle de La Orotava.
I staggered to the sign, then saw it was my head
that said those words; the dwarf, drunk with cava,
me; the tart my double, whereat I fell down dead.

Mannerberefts

An arrogant kind of person
has walked into my house without knocking—
I know a rude two or three—

brash, overweening, cocky,
self-assured, overconfident, cheeky, audacious,
craven mutts stereotypically,

overly familiar mannerberefts
on top of you of a sudden as if owning the place
as if they were perfectly free

to do so, large and in charge,
impossibly smug. I am a formal New Englander.
They *all* hail from Californee.

The Bedruthan Steps

On the cliffs of Bedruthan
I watched the tide rush in:
the coal-black rocks
with heads like forks
of hooded creatures
in exploding percussion
recalling for me my sin.

On the steps of Bedruthan
the spate of cheerless cold
brought the Bronze Age in,
with accusing echoes of sin
along those desolate flats
as the bleak tidal rolled
fetching the without within.

No True Hero Is Part of a Flock

No true hero is part of a flock.
He breasts ill wind like a single knife.
Others prefer to go for a walk.
He confronts singly the maw of strife.

His corvette opts for war alone.
No warrior's thoughts are ever shared.
Group gloating is always a drone.
The moves of a bravo go undeclared.

Coteries revolve in a squirrel cage.
But you find no Achilles loitering there.
The solitary's aim is to disengage,
With no craven coward bending his ear.

The stalwart goes only, solely, and just.
Proceeding unaided is his unique vocation.
Joining's a major assault on trust.
No conjoining for him is not a castration.

North Dakota Tourist Home

Mrs. Roadstead told him, "You're not bringing *that* in here."
It was an old bent fan. Illiterate people are amazingly watchful and
    alert,
and see things literate people miss. Audie Box, a student

booking in, had to be on his way in the early morning dark.
It was a brutally hot late August, and he was suffering thunderstorm
    asthma.
The way you cut your food reflects the way you live,

he concluded, watching the old landlady slice a pheasant—
Confucius believed food should always be served in chopped-up
    pieces,
he knew—a thin, vertical threading, and recalled a proverb,

"Where the devil cannot go, he always sends an old woman."
With paratactic swipes she lopped off the bird's legs and wings,
    fingering
the meat out of the bones she hurled past the fan on the porch.

He paid $2.00 for two sandwiches before retiring to his room.
"You're not bringing a woman in here if 'at's what you think," carped
the lady, noting his bowtie and art book, Venus on the cover,

having formed the strategy of noticing. "I'm nobody's fool,
just because I have no book larnin'," said Mrs. Roadstead taking in
his city shoes, a University of Montana sticker on his luggage,

his aversion to heat. *There is a distinct dysorthographia*
in the flustered way pheasants fly up, Audie Box had noticed earlier,
and breathing heavily with his inhaler trod upstairs to sleep.

Perennial Prejudice

Green and crimson rhubarb
taste pretty much the same.
Kin prefer a different garb,
some selfhood to proclaim.

As fruit stalks tend to ripen
varying colors they undergo,
neither solid or with stripe in
connotes that one stop or go.

Each variety of red, they say
offers a mouth-puckering edge;
green stalks on bright display
are acidic, or so others allege.

Both types offer a detailed crunch,
crisp stalks for gnashing chews,
a chomp, wet snap, a vivid munch
with the tartness of sour ooze.

Toxic is the very nature of *farbe*.
Color bias misperceives.
Still, regarding the species rhubarb,
never, never eat the leaves.

So, what by that is being said?
Go strictly by facts and not prejudice
The first prevents you being dead,
but the latter plain cowardice.

Senator Ted Cruz's Face

What in that rubberized, off-putting quality of a face,
as it smirks, weeps, laments, is so physically repellent

that sycophancy overleaps prevarication? The eyebrows
alone in the sly, downturned look reek of inauthenticity.

No angle of its presentation does not give us the creeps.
Its smarmy smile is death. The ductile lips are bunny-soft

and seem to promise that kind of cold salacious kisses
rapists impose on women they're about to slaughter,

hideously stretched lips, ductile, plastic, inorganic, wet,
yet mealy as a eunuch's spongy front. A grotesque Punch

seems half Judy, as his bent nose meets that upturned chin,
two ugly clowns in one face working to swazzle each other.

Who said it recalled for him the word *Backpfeifengesicht:*
a face in need of a good punch? When he raises his mouth

to smile he has the sly-sheepish look of one caught stealing,
his weak eye-sockets drooping only to enhance his lying eyes.

Cruz's pointed nose is disturbable, poking out like a finger
at what seems to be a reeking smell coming from himself,

one that he alone can detect and is weakly hiding like a fart.
A doughiness that makes pallid and flabby the facial hole

appears to recede in wisdom and worth the closer it comes
in an unleavened, unbaked yeast-blob of sickly, bloodless,

waxen, cadaverous flesh. I saw him once and thought of gum,
and all the properties of its soft, polymer, and resin components.

The Man That Cannot Be Reached

There's a certain man that cannot be reached,
Fed up with society's grasp,
Who sagaciously contrives to go self-impeached,
Fully wary of clutch and clasp,
For having suffered the modern abuse
By telephone, email, computer, or fax,
Letter, cell phone, any probing excuse
Devised by maniacal hacks.

To be at some halfwit's beck and call
Simply by dint of his wish
Is a hideous aspect of urban sprawl,
One's soul to impoverish.
For every modern invention contrives
To force you by diabolical means
To enter wherever community thrives
And clutter your private dreams.

Be inaccessible! Unobtainable! Doff
Your gentleman's hat and say "Screw!"
Howl "No comment! Bite me! Piss off!"
Let one who's available never be you.
For to be procurable is being a slave
Unlike any wise man, out of stock,
Learns by *himself* just how to behave.
No true hero is ever part of a flock.

The digital age has killed us with tactics.
Instagram, Facebook, and Twitter are death,
Splintering human brains into matchsticks
Corrupting our spirit like crystal meth.
The way to survive is kiss off the world.
We are addicted to binges by what we crave.
Punt that welcome mat! Keep yourself furled.
Give all community shit a parting wave.

The secret to joy is to disengage.
Cut free from all contact, influence, sway.
Step out for good from the batting cage.
Refuse to be hectored like common prey.
Slam those fucking doors! Kill your TV!
Yank out the cords of that black telephone!
Pitch that screaming cell phone into the sea!
Let peace, simply peace, be your chaperon.

At the Nedick's Stand in Old Herald Square

At the Nedick's stand in old Herald Square
I saw loiterers and bums, tourists and nuns,
wolfing wieners and even beaners on buns
while a huge orange fountain shot in the air.

Saucy males in disguise with perilous eyes
munched on donuts as they ogled the whores
on the stools in that orange and white décor
were as loud as the niggers standing in doors.

They squeezed a mustard on anything meat
as garish as any of the big Broadway lights.
I heard vile lingo and watched gringo fights
who splashing their drinks continued to eat.

Sods crowded that Formica counter to gulp,
a surface of tangerine as a wild giraffe's tit,
but nothing close to legit as or as brightly lit
as that flat orange slurp with discernible pulp.

Runyon and Winchell and Hellinger drank
the same bug juice that is still being served
at that queer emporium, its counter curved,
to aid the surrounding oaves flank by flank.

Considering crumby Manhattan's abracadabra
I recall more than a high El or Plaza Hotel,
Times Square, or the Fulton fish market smell,
the life-giving plume of that orange Niagara,

and on my deathbed when I'm dying of thirst
more than any grilled frank with a perfect crunch,
trust me, beyond any absolute concept of lunch.
a cold Nedick's squash will find me well nursed.

Shirley Temple's Salary

Twentieth-Century-Fox execs provided Shirley with a scooter,
a doll carriage, tall toys, jump ropes, and games of jacks
because no Yiddish mogul would allow himself to be lax
at screwing innocent child actors out of their spondulax
and inexpensive toys from Marx were far cheaper than a tutor.

Wheatgrass Drink

Taste the lawn in it.
Sense the born in it.
Savor the mow in it.
Flavor the grow in it.
Smack the tint in it.
Relish the hint in it.
Swallow the grass in it.
Follow the sass in it.
Sip the jade in it.
Nip the soft glade in it
Draw the sward in it.
Drink the gourd in it.

Sexual Misconduct

> "Peace, crying crocodile, your sounds are heard;
> Take your prey to you."
> —Middleton and Rowley, *The Changeling*

Alice Hairpencil, student at Phillips Academy,
told a girlfriend, "What would most shatter me

is not to be chosen a favorite of Prof. Bureaux,
who is devoted to all in his classes, although

I am convinced that of everyone in this school,
boy or girl, I am of all others the closest to him."

Yet in spite of the way that her fantasies soared,
over the course of three years she was ignored,

not because he was remotely unkind to the girl
she was only one more pupil lost in the swirl,

except that this highschooler soon felt rejected,
singling herself out from her peers as affected

the most of all in his classes by not finding favor
as the special (even romantic) teacher to savor.

Certain facts, unavoidable, we are forced to relate.
She was short, vegetable-shaped, had never a date,

with a small peasant's body as round as beer kegs
that walked on an unsturdy pair of elephant's legs

whose tread could awaken a local seismologist
confirm even the theses of some abductologist.

She was rude, and dogged, persistent, and weak,
her hair stood a-sprout like a wide broadleaf leek.

No more adamant a creature, if truth must be told
was as importunate as Alice or as close to as bold.

She hounded her teacher, she perched on his stairs,
she sought daily advice, she brought him eclairs,

and in one cryptic mood when filled with amour
once secretly slipped a valentine under his door.

She came by his house, on a window pinned notes,
stalking him the way a fan on a movie star dotes.

She appeared everywhere as if waiting applause;
whenever he turned a corner—lo!—there she was.

The more she came on to him, wearing her heart
on her sleeve, the less (by the rules) he took part,

trying hard to convince her how wayward her goal
and as open to trouble in many ways so was her soul.

He sat with her, pitifully explaining all that he could,
took time to go chastely for long walks in the wood.

Some deep, dark hole in the girl relished rejection
which she nurtured within like some evil infection,

choosing in mind to feel abused like some victim,
as if neglecting her was her teacher's sole dictum.

A sad spell of harassment after graduation occurred.
She went to college, married, as many years blurred,

but for a while she sent him letters of a poisonous sort,
the kind to which only the truly disturbed would resort;

there were late-night calls both alarming and vengeful,
followed by hot tears, guilt, and remorse, yet resentful

enough to put one on alert—but then, a time to exalt,
for then suddenly all dramatic scenes came to a halt.

Forty years passed, quite enough then of nemeses.
Alice H. (and her ghost) had vacated the premises.

But then one day came a telephone call unexpected.
Asked the headmaster of PA, quite cold, and directed,

"Are you Professor Bureaux? I must put you on notice.
You are charged with a crime, sir, (someone wrote us,

thus, to complain) of your sexual misconduct." A pause—
but not very long. His accuser? He knew just who it was.

Villa Islazul

As the sun in Cuba's cobalt sky
scattered sequins on the sea, I ate bites
of wind with the light *brisa*,

cruising the indigo Atlantic
in a waving 3000-mile fetch, tempering
the island's cerulean warmth,

to visit powder blue Bacuranao,
perfumed with morning glories, delphiniums,
grape hyacinths, and harvest bells,

where I sat back in my cyan shoes,
sipping a wet azure sangria with its star fruit
with my dish of blue smoked marlin,

whose eyes—once able to distinguish
various hues to cope with low light conditions
in deeper waters, hunting for food,

unlike gluttonous me in my paradise
of lapis, munching sweet meat with a borage
garnish—can no longer discern color.

Joseph and His Brethren

Joseph in the book of Genesis
guilefully stored all of Pharaoh's grain
when harvest yields were great,

so that when cruel helplessness
arose and famine most exacted pain
he could charge a higher rate.

A Tiger's Stripes Are Flames

A tiger's stripes are flames
burned in its flesh like brands
to meet camouflage demands
and falsely hide a lie it tames.

There is a hysterical beauty
in the way they lick and lap
like a designer's stylish wrap
as if to disguise a tiger's duty,

but when springs the beast
in a burst of smoke, its ire
reveals the fatal bite of fire
to roast its prey like grease.

Captain William Bligh Never Had a Son, Fletcher Christian Never Knew His Father

Captain William Blight never had a son,
Fletcher Christian never knew his father.
Sometime friends as their voyage began,
close proximity soon grew a grave bother.

What mutiny is not an attack on authority?
Insubordination thrives at its beating heart.
A majority gains to overwhelm a minority,
where the goal is to sever and stand apart.

Domineering, Bligh found his master's mate
a prig and by redresses and public reprimand
humiliated Christian who drew upon his hate
and responded with rage at the hour at hand.

Was Freud, psychiatrist, correct when stating,
"Which of us does not wish to kill his father"?
That every Oedipal urge is related to mating?
That between the two tension flares? Rather.

Where did their savage encounter take place
—the locale where fate brought it to closure—
as hatefully each the other tried to outface
in this maritime battle given over-exposure?

It is worthwhile noting in this confrontation
that each sought to master the element there,
where mariners both pursued their vocation
in which psychologically each had a share.

Freud stated males are fond of their mothers,
whomever they seek, to whomever they flee.
Why look for wider examples, though others
may offer any fit nominee? Mother's the sea.

Raymond Chandler's Women

> "Put some rouge on your cheeks. . . .
> You look like the snow maiden after a
> hard night with the fishing fleet."
> —Raymond Chandler, *The High Window*

Raymond Chandler made his women murderers—
in four of his seven novels the dame was a killer.

Beauty blackmails! They weren't summer clouds.
They pointed guns straight at you, midget Lugers,

and they unzippered their teeth when they fired.
Who was it had a mouth like prelude to a scream,

hard as the bluing on the cold .38 she slipped out
with a sly smirk you could feel in your hip pocket,

you in lust feeling bent as a hoop until you saw
her thin too taut lips with an up-from-under look?

Remember her with legs from here 'til Tuesday,
nylons as shiny as scleroderma, lips parted red

as a fire-bucket, crimson fingernails sharp tines
no tigress ever had? Only when a bitch's bullets

hit you was it automatic to comprehend, by what
you mistakenly thought love, she meant business.

The Desert Fathers

John the Dwarf yearned to become an angel.
St. Arsenius would allow no one see his face.
Abbot Pambo ate black radishes in solitude.

They fled the world *not* to be extraordinary,
which in so doing is only to carry the world
with one like a hump for cheap comparison.

It may come as a shocking surprise to learn
that the anchorite St. Anthony, of all people,
thought even Satan had some good in him,

concluding that not even he was purely evil,
since the Father for his goodness would not
create pure evil, for all his works are good.

Those old hermits in their vision well new
that for us, to look extraordinary, we chose
to heap all our own evil upon the "enemy,"

to absolve us of our sins. The desert solitaries
were much wiser, and, for all their black food,
cerulean wishes, and the drive to disappear,

they look odd only to the truly odd, faceless
dwarfs like us who in a deep atrocious black
of our *own* worldly sins inhabit a true desert.

Bird of Paradise

It is a noble queen, of course,
gracious, with the proper words, gently rouged, not roughened,
bearing a notable bourse,

its durable sheath and beak
making a suitable perch for holding sunbirds which pollinate
radiant flowers at their peak,

three brilliant orange sepals
and three petals purplish-blue forming an arrow-like nectary
that conjoin as royal tepals

for flashy birds to sit to drink
its nectar as fronds gently open to cover their feet in pollen
with a grace and favor interlink

as a monarch will commence,
a gracious flower bearing a long stalk like the wave of a scepter,
its sovereign favors to dispense.

His Cremains Will Be Inurned

Of all expressions there are
of horrors to be discerned

doubtless the worst by far,
read on a page quickly turned,

is the funeral announcement
"His cremains will be inurned"

(both verbal and nounal pronouncement)
when a body has swiftly adjourned.

The words are hideous argot,
bleak, formal, and unconcerned,

the cargo a reduction of ashes
so dexterously being returned

in the form of an exequial jug,
$160, actual brass, and ferned.

I picture the corpus dispatched,
so conserved after being burned,

as a cue for me, briskly detached,
to ensure that vile image be spurned.

Speaking of Ozymandias

When a Jewish actor
using a bogus name succeeds,
who then reaps the glory

of his box-office fame?
He'll be reaping the proceeds,
yes, but what of praise

then adhibits to himself,
since all private value recedes,
proving him transitory?

Crane

As a crane bugled sadly across the wind,
I felt a warning to beware,

for it seemed aimless and eerily twinned
with the thin incoherent air,

imparting a black terror that I had sinned,
my poor soul in cold despair.

I Was Looking for Me

> "I am not ghoulish, am I?"
> —Diane Arbus, to a friend

Midgets, nudists, female impersonators,
hermaphrodites, albino sword swallowers

—Arbus called them "fairy tale characters"—
were her subjects, sad, pathetic marginals

caught in that square format, dead-on view,
coldly photographed, the halt and the lame.

She mournfully saw herself in her crippled lens,
looking into an abyss, but seeing *her* reflection,

stirring the toxic brew of humanity for kicks,
but smelling the evil of her own concoctions.

She often visited mental institutions, spying
for the frantic feebles, an incontinent voyeur

who, making much ho-ho-harrowing horror,
selected her sad subjects by what would sell,

never asking their permission, snapped at them
like the mad, sad, avaricious crocodile she was.

Her desperate suicide was her weak apology.
She stole people, rolled people, told people

lies about the fame they would find in pics,
but, feeling guilt, she became her own dwarf,

and so slashed her wrists with a razor, writing
the words "Last Supper" in her diary, placing

the appointment book on the stairs leading up
to the bathroom, to try to wash away her sins.

Someone named Marvin Israel found her body
in a rude bathtub two days later—at age forty-eight—

gone off to a dark eternity only to find herself
with monsters sharing a room with her in hell.

Jehu the Madman

"But Jehu took no heed to walk in the law of
the Lord God of Israel with all his heart: for he
departed not from the sins of Jeroboam, which
made Israel to sin."
—2 Kings 10:31

Jehu well loved his bloody work,
anointed by crazy Elisha to be king,
and not for a second did he shirk

to wipe out the house of Ahab,
raving with a naked knife and sling,
pitiless with every savage stab;

relentless he spiked King Joram,
then raced to butcher Ahab's seventy sons,
mad to have met the quorum,

slaughtered all the priests of Baal,
and any who spoke his evil tongues,
with fury, sword, tooth and nail,

dispatching Ahaziah king of Judah,
then saw Jezebel killed without a qualm
his teeth in her like a barracuda.

He raced madly from victim to victim
on his historic rampage with ringing alarm,
in his mouth an evangelist's dictum.

He exterminated all the living priests,
wiped out sons-in-law, eliminated partisans
of Tyre, annihilating even beasts,

destroying all the temples and pillars
eradicating, as well, all the royal artisans,
shining best of the prophet's killers,

a master of mayhem and massacre.
He thrilled to kill and lived to destroy,
giving murder its greatest capacitor.

Although Jehu was an agent of God,
no faith, no belief had this delivery boy,
a Hebrew hero, but distinctly odd

in that a chosen one of a holy prophet
literally danced to wallow in gore at flood
as if ruled alone by the law of Tophet.

Who is to blame as the king of prey,
this maniac Jehu with hands dripping blood
or Yahweh in all his eminence gray?

Such a mad assassin was Israel's king,
seen on the Black Obelisk of Shalmaneser III,
revered in Biblical glory and coloring,

so, ask yourself when a God's unstable
if the sky's not a projection of human debris,
faith less a matter of fact than fable.

There Exists No Present

There exists no true present, as such.
We know the past merely as a present memory
and any mysteriously opaque future
strictly as present anticipation, a mere
prospect, yet while we have no real present
—for it is fading away like smoke—

we face nothing in fact *but* a real present,
our minds brokering mere interplay of time
in a no-time moment. Present is snatched
by the future, all presentiments included,
and if you choose to look for a further proof
time has already swallowed up this poem.

Mrs. Bindweed and the Poll Tax

Being habit-ridden is a form of crankiness.
Old Mrs. Bindweed in her sitting-room on Bumps River Road,
an area with bogs known as "Hard Dig"

in Old Colony Times, extended harsh marsh,
was determined, spooning from a bowl of codfish and potatoes,
white as spite, not to pay her poll tax—*refused*—

seeing it was only another way to be bilked.
Cape Cod is famously flinty of bush. Spring is ramrod rigid
and wet. Aphra was one who managed to grow

astragulus, comfrey, and bee balm, which served
her teacup and sufficed as well for croup, so let the druggists
be damned, OK? She asked *nothing* of the town,

no water, no mail delivery, no poppets in school.
If she and Eliphalet could go off snap-scooping-up cranberries,
—they fronted bog—feed on tiny cherrystones

by the winter peck, fry up in oil Mashpee herring,
feed their cow black grass, or *wodnocket*, mowed as fresh hay,
walk to farmer's market over at Popple Bottom,

keep a rain barrel, put up beans, corn, and carrots,
pick blueberries and beach plums, *so could the Wampanoags!*
She called the natives hard names, an indolent,

lame, put-it-off-to-tomorrow lot from the backside—
"kill-cows"—who made do with outdoor peg-leg furniture
    they stole!
She laid it all on the sea climate and the heavy air.

Answering a knock, she asked the order man for flour,
butter, a few pickled limes (no wrapping of any kind) to suck,
and corned beef, to use the liquor later for soup.

"So why should a head tax or capitation include them?"
The order man guessed the poll tax was a requirement for voting,
"Wompanigs, too—yup, layabouts, as well," said he.

And could she vote them down, she inquired, vote
that they work? Vote they not assemble on Sundays just to lurk?
Vote they *also* pay, too? The order man said, "Yep."

So, she changed her mind, which was the first time
that she'd done so in ninety-seven years living on old Cape Cod,
down where people of all kinds grew: deaf, cheap,

small, and habit-bound, like the tiny huckleberries
for slump and chocolate-scented daisies, so small now, seemingly
not worth it, yes, where even vegetation is scanty.

Elision

Our three-year-olds howl from the top of their glottal shelf—
typically, in the act of breaking away,
completely in earnest, never in play—
"Noooiiiaaawannandooooitmsyeeeeeeeeeeeeeeeeeeeeelf!!"

Altered Offerings

Chad Slippers always saved the Rooster church
his best offerings for the altar. Irises were his one great love,
despite the fact that people simpered (he knew)

when he primly set them out in cut-glass bowls
on Sunday mornings with the cherishing eye of a true artiste.
He was up at four, using fish-findings for fertilizer.

His was the florist shop in Sandwich on Route 6A,
where he lived alone for years, the one with the mauve sign,
carefully misted his blooms with a French atomizer,

asters, eustoma flowers, wild indigo, verbena, lily
of the Nile, catmint, monkshood, cool sea thistle, candy tuft
crocuses, fuchsia, and thin high-growing clematis,

and wore heavy cologne. He was locally known
for squeezing your fingers for a second when handing you
your change. His glass vases were memorable,

for the rainbow frill. No small shops on the Cape
did well, where even the parishioners seldom stopped in
and the especially unwelcoming soil, stone-beset,

at least in terms of gardening, made it any easier.
Teenage girls would stop in to ask for ferns and giggle,
one lady claimed that his flowers were too bent,

while someone out of who-knows-what motive
mailed him a postcard with the line "Friend of Dorothy."
He was often referred to as a "confirmed bachelor"

by ladies who would nudge each other saying it.
Someone said—gossip was common there—he'd been seen
one dusk at Sandy Neck sitting on a dune, weeping,

looking out to sea, shredding bits of poverty grass.
One fall he strangely disappeared, left to the Poor Farm
his shop with all its goods, flowers, glass bowls,

pots, vases, and all the gardening tools. Someone said
that he had moved to Maine. There would be no donations
to the altar again, not from Chad Slippers' tiny shop,

nor any more irises, for when the adjustors came by
they found that each and every iris had been very carefully
snipped in two and lay on the counter dead.

Henry Thoreau and the Pine Tree

The eastern white pine was Henry's favorite tree,
tall, wholesome, wild, untamed, erect, and round.
He deigned to hug them and by doing so felt free,
standing bold as stalwart soldiers in the ground.
To the aromatic spicy fragrance of its oozy pitch
was resin Henry loved to chew. Its mephitic smell
any true hiker's heart and soul managed to enrich.
Its inner bark is edible when fried and roasted well.
Nothing on the planet stood freer from all blame;
its boughs thrum like harps angelic in the wind,
a symphony mysterious all forests full proclaim
and brought to Henry Massasoit's ghost to mind.
None who comprehend the tree cannot enjoy it,
and swear it ever to preserve and not destroy it.

Stalin

> "I, that am curtail'd of this fair proportion,
> Cheated of feature by dissembling nature,
> Deformed, unfinish'd, sent before my time
> Into this breathing world, scarce half made up."
> —Shakespeare, *Richard III*

Malice is madness and both merciless.
Stalin yearned to be tall with two powerful hands,
according to Shostakovich. Cursedness

left him dwarfish, five-feet-four inches tall
and creepily swarthy, with a pock-marked face.
A boyish accident, perhaps caused by a fall,

made his left elbow stiff, with that arm
foreshortened, making a thick left hand thicker
than the right. So, with dread and alarm

he lived like a partridge hiding his other hand.
He suffered bitterly from vivid bleak disabilities,
which informed his every vicious command.

His second and third toes of his left foot were fused,
as well, unnaturally hideous in an unmade state,
as if some dark fate had made him walk accused,

so maladjusting himself in a perjuring way
he halted gimp through the mad malice he made
to make damn sure well-built others would pay.

Osprey Nest in West Barnstable

The osprey returns on April Fools',
bold with its funny face to squawk.

Its smile is geared for snatching fish,
scooped up in a loop as if by a sock.

As it swoops in with an arc of grace,
it kills by its feet and never its beak.

With its sleek underbody purest white,
most of this hunter is found to be teak,

with a nictating eye of the palest blue,
to squint into the salt sea submersible.

The bird embodies pure concentration,
its yellow eyes sighting straight for prey,

and it aims for the head like a lightning
strike with a fistful of claws on display.

Its prehensile toes are of equal length
with the outer toe quaintly reversible,

(just like the owl's) allowing them ease
to grasp any prey with two toes in front

and two behind, an aid for slippery fish
which describes to a T the prey they hunt.

The back-facing scales on its talons act
as suitable barbs to help hold its catch,

eight sharpened black-as-obsidian knives
perfectly geared to the grasp and the snatch.

It will rarely water-dive below three feet
and loves to nest on man-made structures,

with beds built of sticks and lined with sod,
algae, grasses, any of nature's odd fractures.

It calls *yewk*, *yewk*, its cry when taking a fish
the pierce of a loud, sheet-tearing *chereek*,

which proves more than any example I know
—nature's proof—*joy* can be heard in a shriek.

Toad

Calumniating his mother by telling lies in print,
—after she was dead (it fits the author's style)—
he called his novel fiction but with base intent
manipulated all the facts like a hypocrite vile,
choosing to indemnify by the furthering deceit
of double-dealing falsity with lame half-truth,
as a way to make himself look good yet treat
disreputable invention as somehow solid proof.
This is the way Iago worked, using base denial,
mocking innocence by any facts he had at hand
to cripple decency by innuendo sly, a show trial
crucifying everybody in his artless motherland.
Motives in savage Iago remain immune to wit.
Not so in cane toads—poison's what they spit.

Please Don't Let It Be Gray
(song lyrics)

Let it storm in the morn, let it fever,
Even spates of hail can be a reliever,
But please don't let it be gray.

Mist I can take, gelid weather assign,
The harshest of any whirlwind malign,
But please don't let it be gray.

Stay away charcoal, at least for a week
Nothing gunmetal, I beg, sunless, or bleak.
No, *pleeeeease* don't let it be gray.

Snow, driving sleet, a Punjab-like rain,
a sudden upheaval to wreck the terrain,
Whateversoever but not merciless gray.

Something insidious cohabits in murk,
hides in, resides in, with an unfailing lurk.
So please don't let it be gray.

Refrain:
I can't do cloudy, dull, overcast, gloomy,
anything dreary and somber entomb me

as if to convey sadly that any day slate,
smoky, or dismal determines my fate.

No sky that registers uniform clay
is—never was, *can't be*—my kind of day.

Not today
No ashtray.
No decay.
So, try if you please don't lead me astray.
And please, please, please, please,
I beg on my knees
No, *please*, don't let it be gray!

An Ex-friend E-mailer

"I will *not* be ignored," fumed this tiny bee,
whose stinger he presumed the size of a tree

and went buzzing repeatedly round my head,
but it wasn't so much I considered him dead

—although the pest mattered to me not a jot,
why bother with small, a speck, or a spot?—

but soon disregarding him became my delight,
the perfect squelch for loud pests not too bright

who actually think that they center the world,
and, so, looking past this insect who twirled,

or tried to, around me it seemed day after day
I decided to best him, that the best way to pay

was not to pay heed to his bruit or his buzz
not even swat him—but treat him like fuzz,

for to ignore anyone vain quickly destroys
(and is *the* way to treat) creatures of noise!

Predictably, this dipshit flew off, never fear.
And so, my new dispensation?—*I am not here!*

Poppies in New England

In the middle of ferocious July heat,
wilted and burnt under yellow sky

poppies in the garden are but sticks
dun-brown, fallen, depleted, and dry

as corn shucks in a late autumn field
as if perversely nature itself to defy.

What to us is being said, thus spent,
while other plants bloom, they die?

Who can riddle this nettling irony
with an answer of worth to descry?

The desiccated upright stalks serve
to ridicule anyone who seems to try,

finding in high midsummer what
blooming fertility proceeds to deny.

I see it a corrective, with a flourish
one's dreams become arid as alkali.

Hansel and Rätsel

When a child I was filled in
that in a gingerbread house
built out of baked children

lived a nightmarish old hag
who stank like a dormouse
of cobwebs, rubbish, and rag.

This was the very first image
I recall of the very first story
told of life's ugly scrimmage

and the horrors of this world,
which proved generally gory
as the passing years unfurled.

It set a long pattern of truth,
of just how life came down,
where distress, pity, and ruth

became ruling themes in life
and poor souls wore a frown
of poverty, trouble and strife.

I lived a wandering Hansel
long into my eightieth year
but no mystery could cancel,

no matter my face so brave,
this gnawing, continuing fear
I'll carry with me to my grave.

My Death by Hieronymus Bosch

An endocrine dwarf playing a red fish horn,
blowing his chanterelles,
seemed oddly to convey less joy than scorn,

and as he squatted, jangling round his knees,
ropes of tinny sonic bells
rattled a *chevrotement* in most uncanny keys,

all as if aimed to a single dot-spot in my head
and seeing that evil spells
had chosen me: I immediately fell down dead.

The Sin of Wearing Periwigs

Reverend George Weekes of Harwich, Mass.
was lamenting in 1779 on the sin of wearing periwigs,
preaching that prelapsarian Adam,

so long as he continued in innocency,
did wear his own hair and never a peruke or postiche.
"Is it not within our own small minds,

our skullboxes beneath such foppish wigs,
to find the resolve to put away vanity? Whence comes
vanity? Can the lack of tragedy nowadays

be accounted for by whympering excuses,
the lame plead for by the psychiatric in modern life?"
he railed. He took black Bible in hand

and, waggling it mockingly behind his head
like a bobbing pigtail, leaned forward with his nose
aflame. "If our miseries are born and bred

within our minds, why then heroic action
is impossible. Classical tragedy imagines disasters
as coming from *outside* our narrow selves

—from the gods, from fates, from illness,
from an ancient family curse. Are the squat periwigs
we wear an outside fashion we can rebuke,

or a growth-out, like stolid hair, created
by our conceit, our self-love, vainglorious narcissism
borne of our own weakness, not style?"

He swallowed bile. "Crippledom inside
is no excuse, nor acceptance of some sad visitation
by which fickling fate is blamed, you hear?

Sinners, be no more synthetic! Wage a war
of gravity against your slothful urges! They are all
as full of nits as your resolves. Willfulness

is a wig! Whympering and wit is a wig!
Barber yourselves that the tragic can be overcome
by what real hair covers or pate declares.

Brave men of Harwich and womankind
are not frail, and any loss of innocence is worse by far
than loss of hair or hair of luster. Amen."

The Quality of Mercy

"The quality of mercy is not strained,
It droppeth as the gentle rain from heaven
upon the place beneath."
—Shakespeare, *The Merchant of Venice*

>While millions
>have cringed
>in mortal fear
>of a living Hell,
>
>the final truth
>may be told
>to those awaiting
>the final bell
>
>that in spite of
>all of mankind's
>terrible sins in a
>universe flawed
>
>although Hell exists
>it is kept empty
>by a merciful, just,
>and loving God.

Anxiety at the Blue Mosque

It was suffering from thunderstorm asthma
that in the merciless heat I felt a dark oppressive sense of sky
overmastering my weak aging heart

as I stumbled into a mosque in Istanbul.
A dome has no right, or left, no north or south—it is a symbol
of the limitless vault of heaven—

and instead of feeling undermined or shut in
I felt lovingly, inclusively, spiritually enveloped, aware as I was
of no aisles, or walls. No sense of direction,

no distinction of parts, appropriated my gasps,
diminishing now with the fugue of an increasing sense of height,
so protectively real, when it seemed as if

the Sultan Ahmed, who had worked on it
with his own hands, spoke to me across four centuries, when
suddenly I saw Borak, winged horse

with a woman's face and a peacock's tail,
and there with the Prophet being transported to Jerusalem, where
he met Abraham, Moses, and Jesus,

opening my lungs, clear as the blue tiles
bathed in mystical blue light breathe when, lo, with pure air again,
bright blue, I grew as tall as a minaret.

Venomous Cone Shells

Venomous cone shells
especially *Comus geographicus*, *Conus tulipa*, and *Conus striatus*
can all be starkly fatal.

Abruptly, you can't see,
you cannot breathe, cannot move, but freeze paretic in living stasis,
becoming virtually prenatal.

The Habit of Saying No

> "Poems are about what you don't mean,
> as well as what you do mean."
> —Robert Frost

No—rejection as reply—sits at the direct center of self,
stating a watchword that epitomizes one's essential core

of prerogative, demanding steadfastness and commitment.
One must obey its full resolve. Adam and Eve said no,

So did Eurydice, wife of Orpheus, Lot's wife, Prometheus,
the old Hebrew prophets muttering in their wagging beards.

No is conducive to a person's psychological well-being,
inculcating the invaluable confidence you are not a prat.

It is a boundary, a partition, a strict dividing line, allowing
for individual space, its location its own ethic and aesthetic.

Where an obligation can be quickly slain, freedom may ensue.
I have considered that the deepest dream of a human being

is to fly. What you pass over you repudiate with wings,
choosing a way to feel free, deciding where *you* land.

Refusal is the cry of its own occasion, not grim reality
but reality grimly seen by way of denial. Any determined

position, indicating firmness, shows style. The very act
of spurning acquires, confers, assumes a kind of power.

It gives advantage, bull dominance. A mysterious side
of it solicits mad guesses at your motives; you reveal

a sharpness suggesting acuity, bravado, judgment
power, authority, home rule, command, control, sway,

no small thing in a world constantly barking at you.
Disliking anything has its own distinction, involving

a definite panache. A negative chic attaches to refusing
something outright. Refusal, a firm no, magnificently

offers its own seal of approval: *disapproval.* Allow
infirm others to determine what you do not mean. I

adore the willing rebuff that fractures expectations
and instantly forges your own actuality, like magic!

The 31st of August

"Release first safety, release second safety..."
—*Dr. Strangelove*

The 31st of August has the ring of a bomb,
the phrase, I mean, a hissing fit of derision

like vexation that in a fussy sibilant storm
evokes an echo of something oddly wrong,

for the fizzle, whistle, and wheeze portend
with its spoor—bearing a doodlebug load?—

the distinct threat of a dire promise to end
our lives like a toxic gas about to explode.

An Alias Is a Mask of Pure Deceit, a Liar's Trope

Does Joel David Katz get credit for Joel Grey?
Bernie Schwartz, the character of Tony Curtis?
Whether they are different people, who can say?
Is self-repudiation seriously made on purpose?

Changing one's name is changing one's identity.
Mr. Harry Houdini (who was born Erich Weiss)
surely eclipsed his true self, surely an obscenity,
by transmogrifying an alias into a showbiz device.

Playwright Elmer Reizenstein in terms of glory
achieved nothing on earth of his name to suffice
but with Jews, once again, it's the same old story:
he pathetically claimed plaudits as "Elmer Rice."

The man gave up a job as a law clerk—severity
drove him ambitiously to write successful plays,
but he "shortened" his true surname, for *brevity*,
—a craven lie—yet Reizey as such got no praise.

Crude Melvin Kaminsky is no more Mel Brooks
than Robert Zimmerman is guitarist Bob Dylan.
Face it, Barbara Walters by hook and by crook
is asserting Barbara Warmwasser was a villain,

for renouncing or disowning one's actual name
is shedding the solidest dimension of one's life.
The perfidy lies in that, when sucking for fame,
you have scored out your true self with a knife.

The concept of Ralph Lifshitz from the Bronx
becoming (sic) Ralph Lauren repudiates face,
a family, a fate, a force, and then loudly honks
a contemptuous catcall to mock his own race.

An alias is a mask of pure deceit, a liar's trope,
the persona of a snool who won't reck his rod,
for underneath worldly fame is the tragic hope
that no one will call that fool and faker a fraud.

Dragonflies in Autumn Wheel

Dragonflies in autumn wheel, swirling, swarm for bold aerial
    attacks,
as golden wings flash, blitzing on mosquitoes, butterflies and moths,
snap-snatching at midges in patterns spread as wide as tablecloths,
rotate, spin, orbit, drop, turn, dart, twirl, and whirl on gnats for
    snacks.

Bombers dispatch their flying insect prey by snatching with their
    feet.
Nearly all of a dragonfly's head is eye. No angle (except behind
    them)
can prevent a racing darter-dasher from taking its windy dinner
    neat,
a formal geometry ethereal, if traced, perfect in shape as any diadem.

Nervous Breakdown

I have recently had an occurring mental relapse,
when I decided that all the letters of the Roman alphabet
were in the wrong order, as they are all ranged

arbitrarily, since the three voiced stops, *b*, *g*, and *d*,
are together, as well as the two nasal consonants, *m* and *n*,
but the problem is that the Ugaritic alphabet,

although similar, shows a fricative consonant
between the *g* and the *d*, so the voiced stops are not together
there, while there is a rude non-nasal consonant

between the *m* and the *n*, so that the nasals
are not together there either. The additional consonants
in Ugaritic are consonants which are lost

in Phoenician. So, either the original alphabet order
was that of Ugaritic, or else Ugaritic later inserted consonants
into the order that was found in Phoenician, which

is possible, since Ugaritic also has three letters
which represent the glottal stop followed by a vowel, namely
'*a*, '*i*, and '*u*, so that seems like an innovation,

since the Phoenician alphabet has no vowel letters.
Still, it is not known which alphabet is older. The letter shapes
of the Ugaritic alphabet look very different, since

they are written using the cuneiform method.
The Roman alphabet essentially follows the order of the Greek
alphabet, since it is a modification of that language,

not to mention that it is direct ancestor the Etruscan
alphabet, which follows the order of the Greek, which follows
the order of the Phoenician, of mysterious origins.

The Greek alphabet follows the order of the Phoenician,
since it is a modification of that very alphabet. The reason
for the alphabet order of Phoenician is not known,

for although that was an alphabet of consonants only,
they seem to have been arranged in an arbitrary order. Possibly
there is a little non-arbitrariness in that alphabet,

although it is a well-known historical fact that
the letter shapes of Phoenician are generally similar to Greek,
since the Greeks got the alphabet from Phoenician,

and modified it in part by changing the values
of several consonants to represent vowels instead of consonants.
The letter shapes of the Roman alphabet, then,

are quite similar to Greek, even though the Romans
really got their alphabet from the Etruscans, who in turn got theirs
from the Greeks. I was released by the doctors

last Friday, after being observed for three months
and kept in solitary confinement all the while, because they took it as
a relatively positive sign I began talking again.

Logion

Any two people loving
and agreeing with each other
is church enough,

as it had been for Amos,
a fig farmer, for whom religion
consisted not in ritual

but in righteousness.
Such is true worship. Ceremonial
leave to theologians.

Dick Nixon Was an Endoproct

Dick Nixon was an endoproct,
a man whose anus was inside,
as if to say his bum was locked
in a creature seeking to hide.

Worms are the best examples
of this strange phenomenon;
the sea offers classic samples
of asses faced inward, not on.

"Crypto-bums" applies to them
as they go floating and drift about.
Remember only, seeking stem,
look within and never without.

Toss Pot

A slob daily throws beer cans and little nips
on the front of our property, near a tall oak,
driving by. It is far less habit than obsession.

I can't fail to find him on his passionate trips
less a cretin than some sodden alcoholic bloke
involving me in some odd, warped congestion.

Am I wide of the mark in seeing, as he sips,
he is in love with me? Much stranger folk
inhabit this street, devoted to such ingestion.

Is it not possible by some bizarre apocalypse
that each day is Valentine's for him, no joke,
and courting this way makes its suggestion,

as he drains the drinks from his chubby lips,
that each bottle he flings is a lovelorn stroke
in another desperate try to pop the question?

Archbishop Talbot Blacklaws

Archbishop Talbot Blacklaws, a well-respected
but scrupulous liturgist, on one occasion, an Easter Mass in a niche
at St. Etheldreda's Church in Holborn, London,

indignantly refused to celebrate the service
because the Missal ribbons had been, all askew, imperfectly ironed.
He also demanded perfectly starched surpluses.

"Do not rejoice, Israel," he scolded an inattentive
but shocked congregation, "do not be jubilant like the other nations.
For you have been unfaithful to your God:

you love the wages of the tarts at every cornfloor."
He sipped Hendrick's Gin in private at night and stewed about
    much.
He had a savage dislike of being rained on,

which prompted several curates once to buy him
a woodstick umbrella whose cane of *Viburnum lentago* had a fetid
    odor.
The archbishop's words were like a whipcord

to parishioners who came in late. "Dogsnozzles,"
he snapped at small, inattentive altar boys, and notoriously excoriated
the Act of Supremacy at every waking moment,

pointing out to his "*faux-amis*" that Elizabeth I sinned,
that Westminster Abbey was a monastery stolen, that he wanted the
    Kyrie
intoned, the Latin chant calmly sung, and unaffectedly,

with silence between verses, as the simple sounds
inspired prayer. "Shorten the sign of peace," her barked, choose a
    plainer
"Gloria," and railed against showy recessionals,

wailing, "The goal is to send people out into the world
with a sense of just what took place, with a liturgy of quiet power.
    "God
is not Mr. Disney, the fantastic-realist mythmaker!"

I Shudder to See
My Books Misaligned

I shudder to see my books misaligned
by a heedless hand indifferent to them
—to their different sizes wholly blind—
thicker volumes slopped on top of thin,
stacked backwards, many upside-down,
hindside to, titles on all spines faced in.
illogic in the stack from foot to crown.
Some person, not a reader, piled them
(sole consideration: mass and quantity)
that as a quick assemblage being made
it might be out of sight, with duty paid,
neither a collection nor a treasured lot,
but a stockpile, an accumulation solved,
like vegetables thrown aimless in a pot,
an irritating heap, a mound, a stockpile.
an escalating pyramid, buttload of slew,
very like boulders hurled into a rockpile
calculated by insufferable hands a hoard
of waste the moment they were bought,
things far better out of sight and stored.

Hyperborea

Winter's on its way here without you,
bold with a frost that quotes your eyes
and in the hoary way it whitens skies
and, freezing evening vapor as it dies,
it tasks me to recall the facts I knew

of what so very long I would dispel
of icy memories that froze my soul
like icy gusts from a northern pole
which you embody like the very cold
that is best described by Pluto's hell.

One recalls in ice, as well, its daughter,
you again, weak, in the insolence water.

Heavy Rain Like Mah Jongg Tiles in Thailand

Rain has designations,
I felt, running through a downpour
battle-rattling long
upon the streets in judders.
Chow pung kong
like tiles of wood and bone,
where I was chosen
by lot to be East,
not by a fate I can condone,
except by fate's own reasons.
The violet rain beat
winds and dragons, flowers and seasons,
cracks and dots, and slathers and circles
in a long steady sleet
of surrealist purples,
and in a nearby shed
I went face down like tiles
down-ducking my head
and drawing my hand
through my wet hair and found
despite wet denials
that in the end it had bouquet,
a designation—somehow—
that strangely kept the rain away.

Stanley Pissoir Loved to Obey

Stanley Pissoir loved to obey.
He hoped for school buses to flash their red lights
so that he could come to a stop

to show himself obedient, and,
when wailing ambulances appeared far behind him
with lights blinking on and off,

nothing could make him happier
than to pull his car over, swerving sharply to the right,
off road, to huddle basely in a cringe,

despite the fact that wide open lanes
on the road impeded no vehicle from racing through.
Whenever a cop would raise a prohibitory

hand to stop his car in line, he'd smile
and tip his cap. "Do you always shut off your radio
when heading through a tunnel?"

he expectantly asked me when once
I happened to do so, inadvertently, to concentrate
on something else. "Good. *Good*,"

he said with relief, for conformity,
deep yearnings to show good behavior, took precedence
in his life. Do not merely follow authority—

that was not enough—be *worthy* of it!
This was his ideal, to show how, when asked to lead,
his comfort, his joy, was to follow,

with all his devoutly fascist fiddlings in life
giving him greatest comfort. To comply to commands
were hugs he gave, to demands kisses.

Mermaid Hair

"Mermaid hair don't care, does it, Daddy?"
—Shenandoah Theroux

Peering outside in luscious spring
I see a wet bush damson as grape
like a flaring fairy about to sing
conjoining music, land, and scape,

so, this weigela, a deciduous shrub
with body of spilled-wine flowers,
offering up with each honeyed stub
sweets to buzzing bees in bowers,

proves her dream of mermaid hair,
deepest purple with partial pink,
can be vividly real, and as I stare
at this mane the sylphs will prink

desire these magic locks and curls
to gently fluff with dainty stroke
and by so seducing enchanting girls
make easily real a dream baroque.

Poussin

Poussin took his gods seriously—"a mind
thrown back two thousand years, naturalized in antiquity,"
or so said Sir Joshua Reynolds. There are

no ruins in his work, because for him
the ages past were not a past at all, for he invoked the ancients
as friends. Nor did the Hellenic deities

in his penetrating eyes conflict with God.
To his bold, syncretic mind Christ might well have been the last
of the Greek deities, a latter-day Apollo,

as He appears on early Christian sarcophagi
the painter saw in Rome. He came to nature ready to love it,
fabricating myths he classicized in stories,

incorporating pagan and Christian worlds,
aesthetic and religious beliefs, mountains, gold wheatfields,
gardens, floral scenes, and landscapes,

where gods and prophets met in myth.
Spring, traditionally personified by Roman goddess Flora,
features Adam and Eve in Eden; *Summer*

is symbolized by Ruth in Boaz's fields,
not by Ceres. The sky that empowered Poussin's mind
gave us the Olympian and the quotidian.

"I neglected nothing," said Poussin of his art,
where monster Polyphemus could as easily have wept for Jesus
Crucified as for the absent sea-nymph Galatea.

Aural Symmetry

The word for "economics" in China is *ching-chi*,
as if an Eastern cash register is fashioned to ring

with the typical sound our own does right on key
registering that Western rousing musical *ka-ching*.

Panther Attack in Diyatalawa

A panther hiding in a clump of jhow
with a loud roar leapt its full occlusive black at the disc of sun
in a catapult that wildly matches the arc

of the branching tree a chital deer
crashed under, neckbitten, and one pitifully hears the
sha sha sha of panting, casuarinas

blowing, in gasps between sharp teeth
greenish and almost long as the highlands in Diyatalawa
on the wide-spreading Ceylon tea estate.

It has been said that a terrified victim
actually feels no pain once so fatally caught, but swoons
into the grip of a trance even as it feels

its snout bitten off, the instant shock
proving a natural process while the poor victim is devoured,
thrashing in grass and beefwood cones

with a strapping odor of tamarack rising
in the reek of blood, the very moment its reverberating legs
stiffen, just as the pulsing hot black fur,

bedspreading the willing acquiescence,
ceases its own convulsive gasps, agitations, that submission
has fashioned for only yet another meal.

Death Is Not an Event in Life

"Death is not an event in life; it is not lived through."
—Ludwig Wittgenstein

The bereaved are reminded of their loss by anything that recalls the dead.
Accommodating the realization forces a contrast that foresees a death day.
There is a morbid urgency when something out of life, but in, is put in play.
It is cruel to the extent that forgetting and remembering occupies one head.

The concept of letting go simultaneously involves as memory that's kept.
Whenever we call to mind the dead as dead, we also bring them back alive.
If death is not an event in life, can we therefore by ignoring it then thrive?
Should we the living so regret that, when someone we loved died, we wept.

Nose Twisters

for Katharine S. White

"If a flower hasn't a scent, it isn't worth growing," proclaimed Lady Astor (Nancy Witcher Langhorne Astor, Viscountess Astor, May 19, 1879–May 2,1964), the first female Member of Parliament, who always demanded from her gardener, Frank Copcutt, at her estate, Cliveden, a white flower every day, a fresh one, and it had to be scented.

Don't hand me that crap about fragrance.
You're not walking into Lord & Taylor's at Christmas!
Give me pungent *late* summer flowers,
the small ones, smelling of old jackets—
what compared to the other saints was promised Dismas,
mildly deer-resistant,
nothing too insistent,
something with the hint of vagrance
with the reeky-pee-scent of ancient towers,
the dark wiccan stink of angry pyewackets,
nothing like calla lilies in decadent jackets,
look not at the ceiling, consider the floor,
no noise, tiny blooms, a simple cup,
undeclaring, puritan, unprettied up,
the smug attitude, say, of a closing door:
marigolds, calendulas, chrysanthemums, single nasturtiums,
stenchy, fetid, frowsty, overripe, musty, rank, even irksome,
unfinished, so to speak, blooms still to have some work done
Zinnias heleniums with tawny, golden shades of late autumn
the last wandering stragglers in a parade, lost and so forgotten
their scents still seasoned,
tiny, not overly reasoned,
fall, old shoes, garden-shed-floor.
I choose those and choose nothing more.

As I Rode My Bike from Carondelet

As I rode my bike from Carondelet
I began to hear trees whisper at me
and tried to learn in a knowing way
if from such voices I'd ever be free

and to see what I was trying to be
tried to hear what they had to say
as voices echoed from tree to tree:
you're riding a bike *to* Carondelet.

With horror it suddenly came to me
upon riding my bike to Carondelet
the voices were repeating the plea
that as I rode I rode the wrong way

through *life*, they said, to try allay
the hushed voices disquieting me,
not just bike-riding in Carondelet,
a decree I had long refused to see.

So, I rode my bike out of Carondelet,
after hearing the trees whisper to me,
to heed whatever my voices had to say
and ride forever through mental debris.

O, to Go Home, but Where?
I Was Never There!

In *The Misfits*, frail Marilyn Monroe asks Clark Gable, "How do you find your way in the dark?" "Just head for that big star straight on," he tells her. "The highway's under it. It'll take us home." It wasn't in the script, but the actress hastily added, "Oh to go home, but where? I was never there." John Huston cut her line from the final print.

"O to go home, but where, oh
where? Who'll show me a trace?

Old dreams of never to roam,
which strangely made me race

while born of my deepest fear
served only to hasten my pace,

as if in some nightmare a scare
undefined sought me in a chase

but always left me sadly alone
to wake up in an empty space.

People all tell me to go home—
and, yes, I've heard of the place—

but I was never there, you see,
can't you see, I was never there?"

Islam Loves Sheepmeat

What do they all ponder
who, mowsing hot mutton, pray
to meet their godly duty

in mixing milk with meat?
There is high firmament to fill
for Allah's intercession.

Islam loves hot sheepmeat,
favoring ewes cooked in tail fat
and spit-roasted by night

under a black star-filled
amphitheater of escalating dunes,
supper bleating no more,

throat slit by ritual, bled dry
by way of the sharpest of knives,
hung upside down in wind,

a moist esculent mutton
stewed with yoghurt and cumin,
a deliberate inversion—

aimed at dastardly falasha—
of seething kid in its mother's milk,
and the lone blessedness

of the nomadic tribesman
is that tradition means every much
to a feeding man as faith.

Mr. Wartofsky, the Antique Coin Dealer

No one sang the crap and ruin of our culture
like Mr. Wartofsky, the antique coin dealer

in Mashpee who made it a rule never to have
more than three people standing in his shop

and who couldn't stomach smells of perfume,
which made him the bane of a saving granny

whose Mercury dimes and Franklin half dollars
she tried to sell from a net bag he ripped open,

only to assure her, "Dis is *shrepnel!* Saucepans!
Jack unt jingle!" Had she no gold Liberty Heads?

She believed a dime in her churn would ensure
a plentiful amount of butter that was not hexed!

"Get out!" he screeched at her, her coat smelling
of stinkpot of lavender. The world *plagued* him!

Flies hover near the food, food is always fast,
a house is a tinderbox, and taxes are too high.

The wool we wear is a sponging house, slops
are thrown from cars, and weeds forever win

in whosever's garden. One seaman, a crabber,
pressed a coin into a piece of driftwood and,

letting it float away to ensure his good catch,
blamed creepy Warts of failure, for empty nets.

The world is an inkhorn, blacker than pitch!
All is short commons. "It's all for the best,"

said an old netbag lady, easing shut the door
to the sound of the shop's tinkling cowbell.

"Don't give me that banjo, shit" he bellowed,
closing too early, spitting, yanking the shade,

and, waving off flies, he moped to the back
room to pore over bags of Indian Half Eagles,

minted before the ruin and crap of our culture,
bringing too many *bilixkates* to his coin shop.

The Responsibility of Owning Such a Face

for Shenandoah and Shiloh

"Do you renounce the glamor of evil and refuse to be mastered by
   sin?"
a Catholic is formally asked at any renewal of Baptism, hearing
   within

deeper questions of worth. Imagine for a beauty the force of such
   dread?
A breathtaking woman is open to enticement merely by turning her
   head,

with a face of such extraordinary perfection, it can nature itself
   outpace,
for a burden is born in the terrible responsibility of having such a
   face.

There is a glamor in evil on which evil itself not only sincerely
   depends
but commands a kind of complicity as any friend will solicit her
   friends.

Who would deny that an organ note of power can demolish a
   cathedral,
its thundering echo looping wind through intricate naves
   rhombohedral?

The power of any and all perfection can have consequences
   unforeseen.
Was innocent Eden in its elegantly natural state perpetually
   evergreen?

The apogee, the perfection, of beauty can be tried in an endless pursuit,
daily tested to see from misplaced vanity if compliments still compute.

Sin can master the human heart and lay waste the most innocent dreams,
so insinuatingly subtle, if unheeded, it can reach to the fiercest extremes.

The danger of having beauty is it can feed into the lies that society brings,
which seek the heart of someone's emotions and circle it round like rings.

O, bless the symmetrical beauty you show in the loveliness of your face,
but let it work on whatever you see, and let it always reflect God's grace.

Clive of Warninglid

I remember seeing Clive at Warninglid,
scything the grass in the old churchyard,
stoking it into hayricks, and then selling

the lot to nearby town farmers, as he did.
His wage was merely a quid a week, hard
money. He was hit by lightning, yelling.

They found his flagon at The Giant Squid,
gave it to the rector without special regard.
No one's tears at his wake needed quelling.

Reflections on One's State

I hate a nosy personal question.
It gives humans too much importance.
Everyone is by far too vain.

Reflection on one's state
makes for futile and merciless egotism.
It will drive you insane.

Introvert questions pall.
They all center arrogantly on the self.
Worship no one's brain.

We are all of us solitary.
The attempt to be imperishable is sad.
Remake the world, again.

One seeks publicity and fame,
morbidly asking questions of himself.
Coddling an inner self is inane.

Cooperate with bettering life,
never the fascinations of what you do.
From dreams of glory, abstain.

Treasure sacredly the instant.
Correct and aid what you see outside.
You link a continuous chain.

Make no quoin in any arch
the creature you insist on being big.
Yourself is man in the main.

Table Mountain in Cape Town, South Africa

Looking up at
the height
was not what made me scared.

It was seeing
the *rim*
of the long rock that I feared.

To walk along
the extended
lip of that thing I never dared.

The Silversword Plant

The silversword plant
grows with no flower
until just before it dies

when it fairly explodes
a purple-yellow flower
and expectation defies.

Breaking Waves

When combers roll in doing a logarithm, each wave is built up by a
    backwash of the one before it
until a next moment comes when the tall advancing wave can climb
    no higher, undermined by
the undertow, it curves forward to collapse on the waiting shore with
    a splash,

to slip back on a sliding break as if memory coming alive prepares
    for a crash,
receding in whitish foam while changing to dark greenish colors like
    a drag on a sand-blind lie,
pounding the shore in thunderous brine comes another wave as if to
    outrun and further explore it.

John Profumo Cleaning Toilets at Toynbee Hall

"On 5 June 1963, John Profumo. Secretary of State for War, was forced to admit that he had lied to the House of Commons over a sex scandal with Christine Keeler, an unforgivable offence in British politics. He resigned from office, from the House, and from the Privy Council. Before making his public confession, he confessed the affair to his wife, who stood by him. It was never shown that his relationship with Keeler had led to any breach of national security. The scandal, however, rocked the Conservative government, and was generally held to have been among the causes of its defeat by Labour at the 1964 election. Macmillan had already gone by then, having resigned in October 1963 to be succeeded by Alex Douglas-Home."

—*The Times of London*

John Profumo cleaning toilets at Toynbee Hall,
a charity based in the East End of London, where he continued to work
for the rest of his life, gave him a saintly grace.

He vanished into London's East End for forty years,
performing quiet good works, had to be persuaded to lay down his mop
to lend an equal hand to run the benevolent place.

All of his servile work was done as a volunteer,
to pay for his public sins, and he only occasionally appeared in public
when failing in health, in he was wheeled in a chair.

He was an aristocrat, OBE, landed in Normandy,
but he was honored more by far in the kindness he tendered to others
than, when equally brave, he fought as a brigadier.

I Love You the Way It Rains Diamonds on Jupiter

for Shiloh and Shenandoah

"We shall find peace. We shall hear angels.
We shall see the sky sparkling with diamonds."
—Anton Chekhov

I love you the way it rains diamonds on Jupiter,
a stratospheric lightning bat-scorching methane
always present in the atmosphere, transforming

the odorless, colorless gas into soot, *carbon*! As
clouds of the wild black carbon go raining down
on the big planet, they clump together and form

graphite which gets subjected to intense pressure
from the atmosphere as it gets closer to the planet's
core and transforms into the shiny precious stones

that we voraciously call diamonds. On another orb,
it rains hot glass, sideways, yes, in howling 7000
kilometer-per-hour winds. Such is my love for you.

Capitalism

Business is a savage place to serve God
but yet a capital one to serve mammon,

troublesomely apt a truth for a Christian
for whom any thievery is a flagrant sin.

A heart that grows hard as crucible steel
while it never fits the human soul within

yet does not quite sate the businessman,
craving more pork on top of gammon.

Time Is Money

Nothing on earth
can possibly exceed the joy
of having a rumpy

little four-year-old
daughter in flannel pajamas
wobbling into bed

with you with hugs
and then sleepily answering
with her sweet breath,

when you ask her
with a kiss what time it was,
"$200 dollars!"

Rhino the Gardener

The rhino shits seeds in its dung,
landing in the perfect seed bed, its own wastes
of fine-grained midden mud, a soft embalmer
and therein lies a most curious catch:

he plants his own garden among,
and with, the vegetables that match his tastes,
as precisely those selected by a keen farmer,
pondering what to grow in his patch.

King Louis XIV

Being a king shocks the self,
dramatizing the menacing dragon he has to become
to reign, facing black fears

he is unqualified. It depletes
and angrifies and confounds the way entrapment
fogs the head. A young prince

bowed before and curtseyed to,
even at the age of three balloons into any monster.
The hairdos of powder, power, alone

must be chosen to show bigness,
pressing into the brain the dreadful unavoidability
of waxing large as all others wane,

and so he is positively unable to be
benevolent while also the superimportant firedrake
that shells out rules and regulations.

War was my sole *métier*, the high fee
that makes the mix of commerce, revenge, and pique
that shapes any shockéd king unique.

An Old Ball Mason Teal-Blue Fruit Jar

It had the widest of a wide mouth,
stood squat and solid and teal blue,

with a sleek slope-shoulder design,
a ball zinc and porcelain lined cap

or maybe sometimes a pewter lid
that anyone could screw on tight

in three comforting solid swivels,
manufactured for a hermetic seal,

with a screw-thread that, sturdy,
imparted heft to it like a demijohn,

bottles with rich, embossing bold,
raised, engraved, separate letters

its soda-lime glass stippled in sun
shimmering bright the way a slant

of light ripples on a store window.
It dominated every farmer's shelf,

it preserved, it sealed, it shone—
it was as it stood a real fruit itself.

Princess Grace of Monaco in the Rain

"When told that her marriage had been described as a 'fairy tale romance,' she responded with, 'I've never seen anything fairy tale about it, no.'"
—J. Randy Taraborrelli, *Once Upon a Time*

Grace Kelly did not enjoy the sun,
and never had. "I prefer the rain,"

she said to a friend in Monaco, one
whom she knew could feel her pain.

"Why God put me here," she added,
"I don't know." She kept sunglasses

everywhere, preferred staying hatted,
fearing even corroding solar gasses.

A heliophobe avoids sunburn, light,
taking comfort in clouds, overcast

days that temper anything bright,
which involved her job, harassed

as she was by all the glitter and gilt
that mounted to a sort of persecution

she suffered over decades to the hilt.
The dark became her sole solution,

anodyne to hot blistering beaches
on which selfish playboys lounged,

under the violet sun rays' reaches,
in Speedos, decadently browned.

Cloudy, murky, leaden, gloomy,
misty, hazy, dismal, dark, spumy,

shade and shadow gave her back
herself, sheltering from the glare.

It does not fit to find in any royalty,
where sunshine, daylight, solar rays

virtually define their regal loyalty,
a princess who abhorred their gaze

and chose to shutter from the sun.
Her sad confession, born of strife,

was by a crown was nothing won
and she now rued her choice in life.

Honoré de Balzac

Balzac who hard coaxed
his words to produce fat material that passed
through violent processes

which had small chance
of any delicate finish in that urgent fierceness
wrote like a plant explodes,

a Mediterranean squirting cucumber
bursting from its stalks to shoot through the air
or broom, powering its explosions

to detonate like a shooting pen
to go splattering black seeds in all directions,
eruptive outbursts, making art.

Asseroe in Ballyshannon

"The beauty of a landscape resides in its melancholy."
—Ahmet Rasim

Asseroe, Asseroe, near the waterfall
in Ballyshannon, where beautiful mystic voices
lured Rúad to his death in a cascade,

perpetuated in a gray overhang of fog,
blesses the spot where the last of the holy monks
were driven out of the crumbling abbey,

and all that remains now is the west end
of the church, a piece of gable, as time debunks
even the solidity of flinty Gaelic stone,

where I sit on a section of south wall
and ponder, cold in my coat, what the choice is
when I realize how eternity is made.

Logic and Truth

"Christ crucified was truth nailed on
the boards of logic."
—Nicholas Berdyaev

Logic
a faculty too easily
contorted by evil,
is, compared to truth,
an insinuating weevil

Truth
never reckons gain
as the primary goal
but works to discover
the worth of the soul

Logic
discovers nothing
but, like arithmetic
crunching numbers,
is coldly syzygetic

Truth
reaches past reason
by harmony is awed,
firm in every season
fails apart from God

Parson Mullinex's Glebe

> "They wandered in deserts and mountains
> and caves and holes in the ground."
> —Hebrews 11:38

A parson walks along his glebe,
praying above the wheat, which is a revenue in grass,
very like the tiny tithes he collects,

and in his gaiters, buttoned up the side,
Reverend Mullinax swings a stick at thorns, pokes it
through a rabbit-hole, pondering

the vicarious effects the furlong brings
by way of a small collation his neighbors envy him
for having. But how big, how cushy,

is a benefice to an incumbent facing
no end of chancel repair and broken rooves of slate,
an orphan fund, penurious sodalities,

to say nothing of the undrained water
gathering in this sunken ground or this warren of
breaches, breaks, a fallen garden!

The parcel is invaded by burrowers,
not unlike the perpetually attendant parishioners
and their requests in generalities.

There's a burrow, there's a den, a lair
gopher-wide—pit, depression, indentation, hollow.
Can't the things find *another* glebe?

Open fields beckon but the chance
to walk by day with a pace worried deliberation
makes only slow and ponderous

and empty, like holes burrowing foxes
and hares wilily dig up who are also eating up his
rightful proceeds; still along his glebe

he walks, meditating on the meadow
by way of stick-spelunking gaping holes, dunked
hideaways for groundhogs, vagrant voles,

the ruinous beasts, fallen all, making
ankle-breaking ravages where no prebendary,
—and the Messiah would be a priest,

as Hebrews points out—deserving
of his state, and somewhat strapped, needs be
reminded, only yet again, of Eden lost.

Cormorant

> "How like a fawning publican he looks!
> I hate him for he is a Christian."
> —*Merchant of Venice*, 1.3.38–39

Shylock is not and never was a Jewish name.
There was never a Jew named Shylock anyone ever knew.
Any ugly grasping Lombard chewing his cud

under any cloth yarmulke can claw like a raptor,
lending out gold ducats. Shakespeare's usurer's name, adopted
from the ancient Hebrew word *shalakh*,

is taken from a bird of prey (unfit for Jewish diet!)
the red-eyed cormorant gobble-swallowing fish in greedy fits
or any such black shag detested in Leviticus

among kites, bats, ravens, herons, hoopoes,
owls or mad voracious hawks, but all cormorants and darters
have a unique bone on back of the skulltop

known as the *os nuchale* or occipital style,
the so-called xiphoid extension becoming a vital attachment.
This bony projection, like the comic *kippah*,

—for it closely parallels that brimless cap
or circular beanie that bearded haklachic authorities demand
all male yehudim sport to risk ridicule—

provides anchorage, indeed, very like
a Hasidic identity, for the muscles that increase the force
with which the lower mandible is closed

in the same way the highly developed
muscles enclosing it, also empowers a creepy money lender
the chutzpah to be willing to kill for cash.

Four-Year-Olds Talk Like Laurel and Hardy

to Shiloh and Shenandoah

Four-year-olds talk like Laurel and Hardy,
precisely and slowly and fussy and earnest,
pacing out words, concerned, slightly tardy,
with serious stress underlining the sternest.

What by obvious logic needs to be settled
prevails, but in the matter of interruptions
each speaker, huffing, gets visibly nettled
by the off-putting fact of nutty deductions.

One of the two offers long explanations,
while the other, confused, not fully sold
on the accumulating, weird accusations
or the slavish matter of abiding a scold,

exhales with huffs and a scratch of head,
dandling fingers on the top of her crown,
questions the nature of what's being said
not without an open but quizzical frown.

Thus go their exchanges perpetually held
in plain discussion or down-and-out spats,
endless engagement never quite quelled—
the only thing missing is two bowler hats!

Conundrum

> "Never stand where I tell you to stand!
> You stand where I tell you!"
> —W. C. Fields in *The Dentist*

I hate people who do not forgive,
so, am I forgiven for what they have made me feel
in my responding unforgiveness?

Isn't the problem oddly combative
when as a response we harden ourselves like steel
in a plea for others' resistiveness?

John Wayne Slings the Bullshit in *Red River*

Tom Dunson is a selfish brute who fought not in the Civil War,
matching Wayne who spent WWII in the cushy armchair corps.
He tells Matt when drawing a gun, "Watch his [enemy's] eyes,"
when the fact is it's the moving *hands* that cannot be disguised.
He barks orders to all of his cowboys with egotistical disregard.
and has Groot call him *Mr.* Dunson, a typical bossy blowhard,
although they both have suffered together, decades in and out,
with one doing the servile work for the other ass-kicking lout.
He steals Mr. Meeker's herd and Diego's land without qualm,
heedless of whatever he does or to whomever he brings harm.
He idiotically claims there's no market for beef in all of Texas,
commonly known as the state with exactly that national nexus.
He ignores the death of a girlfriend, Fen, deserted as if shoved,
farcically claiming that she was "the only woman I ever loved,"
nor does he go back to bury her but leaves her to desert beasts,
for arrogant bullies find weakness in love, respect, and retreats.
He shoots dead a simple Mexican who asks he leave the land,
watching the gun (not the eyes) held in that *caballero*'s hand.
Hypocritically pious, he attends to every man that he's killed
by asserting "I'll read over him," as if a holy minister skilled.
He does not complain when Matt and Cherry fire off 16 shots,
although cattle never stampede, but a bloke rattles some pots
when stealing a finger of sugar and then panics the entire herd,
then Dunson sets out to whip the man, cursing with every word.
The hideous truth is Dunson is clearly a John Wayne persona,
the latter the movie-star bravo, the film role his lackey corona.
There is not the trace of the hero in either man, merely a bully,
where Wayne is the rope sadistic, and Dunson, his pliant pulley.

Constant Is Neither the Nature of Wind

Constant is neither the nature of wind
nor the fickle, fluxioning state of the female heart
for both gust and lull, back and veer,

can shift in a second, bind and unbind,
never for long, incoherent, rule without fit or start,
without the remotest contours of steer,

will blow to the east an air that's thinned
or cant to south or north with an inexplicable dart,
trackless, desolate, fierce, empty, shear.

Where irrationality is therefore twinned
like women and wind, unable to be decided apart,
an anxiety sits even mercy cannot bear.

Mental Asylums Carry Terrifying Names

Mental institutions bear terrifying names,
scary lockups like Creedmor and Danvers,
Stonehurst, Byberry, Bellevue, and Scanvers,
Overbrook, Koi Pond, the Michigan Tames,

Purdysburn, the Grace of God, Springland,
Lokopriya Gopinath, North Gripsholm Inn.
Broadmoor Hospital, the high security bin,
in the village dorp of Crowthorne, England,

Beechworth, Drakin Acres, Scalebor Park,
Stillwater, Hellsdeon, Truro, Narrenturm,
Bridgend, Whisperwood, and Bannockburn
Orphanborn, Mapperwily, Arkham Stark,

Cane Hill, Goodge, Wenlock Sanatorium,
Gonjiam, Darkbridge, Coppice for Paupers,
Emporium, Weeds, the Grassland Croppers,
Dismas House, Looncall, Dimlet Emporium,

the dark Trans-Allegheny Lunatic Asylum
for Schizophrenics, bipolar, depressive sorts,
haunted buildings with barbed-wire courts
for zomboidal vegetables of every phylum.

Even worse evocations go by Silence Lake,
Sunrise Grove, Sage Forest, Tranquil Falls,
Blissful Heights, Jonquilia, Serenity Halls,
Hospice of Peacefulness at Placidity Lake,

all said to be haunted by malevolent ghosts,
in revenge for shock therapy, frozen baths,
wet sheets, shock therapy, orderlies' wrath,
full-scale lobotomies by mendacious hosts.

I am told everyone has a whispering gallery.
No, I lie, but in a horrid pause one can hear
curses from souls, "Who locked me in here—
Don't the names *prove* their total quackery?

La Ferte

An illustrious forbear of mine, a bravo
in the pioneer entourage of General Lamothe-Cadillac,
and associated with the fur trade

in the wilderness of rustic Detroit,
was named Antoine and by men referred to as *"La Ferte"*
for his temper (or had he red hair?)—

that is Antoine Laumet de la Mothe,
Sieur de Cadillac, governor, explorer, adventurer, founder
of Detroit and Governor of French Louisiana.

My ancestors were a full part of the discovery
of Michigan and later grew up with the Menomenee, as close
to them as these historic words I proudly write.

Nothing is crystal clear about the ethnicity
of my patron or of his wives; but many no doubt were Indians,
given the very few women in New France.

Unlike most Norman settlers, he came
from inland Toulouse, was a marine, spoke a serious French
not of the standard kind, being from the south,

namely Gascony. Speaking Gascon, in fact,
alone would have set him apart gathering pelts or fighting
renegades—Hurons, no doubt. I can feel

the company of both Antoines, Theroux
and Laumet de la Mothe, as I walk through, slog through,
this life, portaging over swamp and slough.

Circularity of Mind

Our circularity of mind
looped in the brain pan
makes reality circular,

so, when closing to bind
all stays finite we scan
in a skull inopercular.

Larry Nassar the Pedophile

"Lord, if you mark iniquities, who shall stand?"
—Psalm 130

Nobody is fully a monster.
Pedophiles are just about the last sad group
that everyone can hate,

left, right, and center,
and despising such men infuses cruel delight
into the judging souls,

who feel much cleaner now,
polished with virtue by being a dark pointer,
barking with rectitude,

jingling with the thrill
of another crucifixion ("Raise him up!
Nail the bastard high!"),

shoving hard to get up close,
faces twisted in merciless condemnation.
Offer mercy to the whales,

the piping plover, pandas,
but keep *that* little pervert in the center light,
watch him go weeping wet

into measureless darkness.
Screw forgiveness! *Who gives it to me?*
I am at best myself and freest

screaming like a loud siren
in my personal Salem courtroom at long last,
a monster to despise—*not me!*

Clap him into an iron jail for life
until the perv goes stark staring mad so that I,
utterly blameless, can feel free.

Dialogue of Self

Two keen rivals in unselfishness competed,
one of whom said he'd prefer to be cheated

in debate and in business than be the cheater.
"You'd rather be the beaten than the beater?"

asked the other, ill-disposed in making room—
"rather than be *who* you'd prefer to be *whom*,

choose to be the put-upon and not the put-ter,
booted like a football, never to be the footer?"

"The lover is more virtuous than the loved,"
came the other's response, seeming the dove.

"So, the lover therefore is the one who *acts*?
Then doesn't that include the cheater? Facts,

your own, seem by far to serve me better,
the gotten the greater loser than the getter."

"But since a lover seeks to give, not take,
he avoids committing a greater mistake,

for the passion to win, in egotists' creeds,
allows higher honor in that one who cedes.

Love acts to give and cherishes that debt.
No force as virtue has been invented yet.

Any pliancy of soul a push has prevented.
Virtue as thrusting has yet to be invented.

The beater, the cheater, the footer are fools,
workmen pathetically no better than tools."

"You win the argument—concede I will,"
says the rival, with a wink. "End of drill."

"Your need to concede is aggression *itself*,
provoking both of two halves of a self!"

So, conceding is winning, and victory loss?
Giving is taking? And crissing is cross?

Both rivals laughed and continued in kind,
sensing the forum of battle a single mind.

Looking at Corot Landscapes in Widener Library on a Dark Rainy Afternoon

Corot's Italian views rarely contained people.
I would choose to live there, far away from all

dumbledores, big hewers of water, neighbors,
groups, over-the-fence-peepers, all the greeters

and bleaters in caps you see at the post office,
pie-faced carpenters, human octopi reaching

out, all those waving meanderers and muttjacks
who daily remind me, like a gong, that, it's true,

the price of free time is indeed eternal vigilance.
On this day, I treasure silence and prefer to leave

merrifying and head-bobbing *meums* and *tuums*
to all howler monkeys who love to gather to gab.

I see myself, all alone, at the edge of the woods
where many a figure sits or wanders in a ponder

in his paintings. Lake Como prompts visitors,
for sure. Here in a library on a rainy afternoon.

I yearn to enter *View from the Farnese Gardens.*
Ponte Narni. Lake Piediluco and Mount Sora,

green solitudes of Ariccia and Terni, Olevano
and the Campagna. The pastoral peace of trees,

rocks, are an unrecoverable past where I sit,
content, nevertheless, and warm for the 1820s

because Corot in his brushy dreams, vigilant
with his dreamy landscapes of bushy greenery

has allowed to be alone with no one's permit
to enter, to interrupt, to intercept, to intrude.

Fred Astaire and Latin Lovers

Alberto Beddini, a dandified Italian fashion designer in *Top Hat*, challenges gay dancing Fred to a sword duel with farcical éclat—whatever door our hero opens there the outraged bantam hovers!
Fred Astaire was ever plagued in films by swarthy Latin Lovers.

Ricardo Romero, the bandleader in *Swingtime*, all cool panache, woos Penny (Ginger) with a plethora of pure Mediterranean tosh at every turn both to best Fred and get her underneath the covers!
Fred Astaire was ever plagued in films by swarthy Latin Lovers.

Rodolfo Tonetti, professional co-respondent in *The Gay Divorcee*, stirs the mix of adulterous machinations with Fred the addressee and speaks with a tongue of butter much smoother than a glover's.
Fred Astaire was ever plagued in films by swarthy Latin Lovers.

The Cranes of Binnalhyuk

Rare endangered red-crowned Manchurian cranes symbolize good luck—
in the waving wetlands that border high misty mountains in Binnalhyuk.

I saw seventeen of them flying, their sword bills an olive-greenish horn,
their legs slate to a grayish black, through pellucid air on an early morn,

to alight and begin a stately dance to *guqin* music with a wind from trees,
fairy their footfalls, thin as winter air, they paced the light evening breeze,

nodding for me to ride on their backs as I watched their graceful pavane
to and fro, a rounded binary, short steps, in tempo, with all delicate elan,

so, I singled one out for the simple beauty of the bare red skin of her crown
and slid my arms around her long black neck with feathers of softest down,

then into the skies we flew, soaring strange clouds, and onto a bluest pond
where she took me with all the flock to wade in a whoopering lake beyond.

They ate rice, parsley, water plants, carrots, buckwheat, hard acorns, frogs,
and stabbed sharpest beaks into carps, snails, dragonflies, reeds, and slugs.

I decided by choice to fly with these cranes into eternity, now and forever,
becoming the eighteenth one of the group, my life with mankind to sever,

for I felt as I rode the groundswell that day to say bye to my human past
and to rise high in the upwelling upsurge and to become immortal at last.

Napoleon in Three Steps

A mere lad attacking
snow forts at school in Brienne,
true martial origin.

A first commission,
quelling local food riots at Lyons,
a budding Achaian.

A defiant general,
leading an army that no quarter lists,
victory at Austerlitz.

Nectar for Pollen

for Richard Attenborough

Said plant to bee,
"Do come a-callin,'

sip all my nectar,
gather my pollen."

"I will get drenched
here on my stinger;

yet all floral sweets
induce me to linger,"

bee stated to plant,
sup-supping away,

"the more you offer,
the more will stay."

Nodding, the plant
said, "It's fair swap.

Whatever I spill,
up you can mop.

I'm only grateful
you will dispense

my personal grains
so free of expense

in simple exchange
for a taste of honey,

a barter of equals
with no use of money.

But do let me ask
who is the male,

me offering juice
or you who impale?"

The Unbranching of Reverend Hole

Rev. R. F. Vercingetorix Farnum Hole,
a curate, vicar, and squire of the Bixby church,
whose vigorous enthusiasm for orchids

showed him great alike in the rectory,
as well as in the bothy, in which woodland hut
he puttered about with farmery dreams

to make drawings of *Cattleya* Queens,
pink *Rhyncholaeliocatt*, Empress Fredericks,
and Hermine in subtle blushing beauty,

fumbled with his prized pastel crayons
which he cherished like a wood pigeon its acorns,
but now on Sundays he would turn up late

too often for services he needed to lead,
explaining, "I'm like a palm tree, I do not branch,"
which cost him his job at a parish meeting,

and so sent down from the Bixby church
he would move up to Scotland to live like mole,
"no better sanctuary for old Reverend Hole,"

as he told it from the pulpit on parting day,
holding up several sketches of work he had done
to three lone parishioners sitting a-bench

on a cruelly cold winter eve, as if to say,
flowers I've turned for glory to worship the Son
and adding, as his heart gave a wrench—

"By 'I do not branch,' I meant to say,
as I told a weeping old lady after Advent mass,
my faith alone is by personal trace"—

he lifted up crayons to a high stained glass,
saying that deep need for color illumined his faith,
that his drawing with love developed grace,

and he left that day with his orchid dreams,
alone, after placing before Christ's crucifix wraith
three cut-out sketches in a wobbly vase.

Who Would Deny the Well-Fed Warble?

Cedar waxwings, no lilting songsters,
gobble in the cold to the music of need, wherein greed
always has a share. In the high branches

I have seen berries of mountain ash
slurped away by these fruit fanatics as if vacuumed,
the birds virtually burping excess

after rapid digestion. They always gorge
themselves to the very throat, stuffing themselves full!
Their song is eating, their burping

response a hushed whistle! Cedarberries
are a waxwing staple. Cherrybirds on salty Cape Cod
love crickets, crane flies, lacewings,

but so overfond of cherries are they,
their fleshy drupe, those shining binnacles of red
so wild, sweet, raw, negligible of fat,

their wee delirious pits sour and tart,
make the bird go *bing, bing, binging* with delight
until there is such a lilt in the gobble,

an incantation of final fart and fission
that it is no surprise a final fatness creates a trill
for who would deny the well-fed warble?

Eutychus Raised from the Dead at Troas

> "'Don't be alarmed,' Paul said. 'He's alive!' Then he went upstairs again and broke bread and ate."
> —Acts of the Apostles 20:10–11

In a window young Eutychus
fell to sleep during a sermon,

as he sat listening to St. Paul,
a man quite fully determined

to bring to any subject at hand
a pious and requisite learning;

long was his homily, warring
on laxity, sin, and like vermin.

At the end of the preachment
just as he brought it to term in

the way of completion he did,
a heavy crash was the burden

felt when out pitched the lad
—a noise so oddly uncertain—

from the tip-top of three-story
building, the highest exertion,

where he lay provably dead,
silent, lifeless, unsquirming.

Out ran the loving preacher,
than whom no better person

lived, to hug the lifeless body
in a grasp of loving coercion

to carry the lad back upstairs
when, so goes every version,

Eutychus came brightly alive,
no longer in pain or hurting,

and they shared a long meal
with a joyous extra serving,

even talking late until dawn,
where Acts draws a curtain.

Mr. Jessup

We had already paid for a crescent window
to be placed on a front of our barn: rejected

by the Cape Cod Historical Commission who
claimed it gave out the wrong "look," despite

the fact that all the revered houses along 6A
carried the very same style that we'd chosen.

Angry Mr. Jessup, bristling, took high offense
that we blithely presumed without permission

to order anything, especially a $650 window.
"You're a thousand miles from the cornfield,

bub," he muttered, not bothering to look up
over half-glasses but merely slid papers by.

He sucked his teeth, fished for small crumbs
between his teeth, wore a fat aluminum watch.

It was a boon for him to preside over applicants
in the last gear of certitude, the better to hector

them about rules. A kleptopredator he loved
to steal your meal and eat you, too. To *prevent*

alone made his day, being the blocking agent.
"Scrabbletown we ain't, OK? Go down island

for that. No water-bewitched porridge here,
mister. No wickie-wackin.' No whole tote."

Dyspeptic, stupid, rude, overbearing, and fat,
his oversized belly matched his circle of hat.

No bigger blowhard can be found than local
commissioners of small affairs. A low level

architect, he loved blocking projects, voting
down additions, widow's walks, paint colors,

public Christmas crèches, disallowing any
and all access roads to be paved, new parks.

I had seen fat Jessup once at the Barnstable
County Fair in his billowing walking shorts

handing out ribbons to prize cattle, his wife,
a heifer, slap-applauding a civic importance

she felt he showed in vetoing odd windows
that were not up to code. It was under a tent.

"That's an *Aberdeen* Angus." I'd corrected him.
"Folks wrongly call them Black Angus," I said

—I know livestock—at his dumb misattribution.
Standing nettled among Shorthorns, Herefords,

the fat judge scowled, but remembered my face
later and brought me low by petty proscriptions.

"So, no re-applications, jasper," he harumphed.
"You'll only be fillin' your belly with east wind.

I've had other Harvard people breezin' in here,
too, cuttin' corners, actin' spleeny. Vinyl siding?

Scrote windows?" He back-hand-slapped papers.
"No purchase, nope! Whole 'notha set of cobbles!

Cut your sail according to your cloth. Wishin'
isn't doin' on Cape not here, not now," he barked

as we leaped up to show him several new photos
to try pleading our case, "Get a transom window,

or be fined!" Two borborygmi. *Or. Be. Fined.*
No load of cork-stopples to be had here. So—

rejected," he quacked, loudly rubber-stamping
three mimeographed sheets. *Bang! Bang, bang!*

Late that night he felt a deep, angry satisfaction
in his bed, the closest the man could feel to glee.

Woodpecker Drumming

Woodpeckers are not singers.
No, their bills are the equivalent of drumsticks
whacking out a rolling tattoo.

As sturdy as human fingers
their rigid pointed tail feathers like solid picks
assist them in what they do

by maintaining like zingers
what keeps them balanced, a perpendicular fix
for any rough bark they hew.

Storge

There is a thrill when you pick up your toddlers from daycare, dramatic, intense, never mild. It almost hurts, the love you feel. To explain the ardor, anticipation will not suffice, nor high zeal in your mind. It speaks rather, uncannily, of your soul laid bare.

The nearly incapacitating wound has roots in the kind of quake that posits a sense of loss in the sad, wayward world that steals and leaves at the core of all passionate love a concomitant ache in the heart of vehement terror that horrifies more than it heals.

Night of the Screech Owl

Of the screech owl
with hectoring scold
carking its eerie voice of terrible horn,

why should not
one's blood run cold
upon hearing its falling note of scorn,

the quavering tones
from an abject wold
framed as if to do little but forewarn,

when we know
its beak stronghold
has shredded mice into seeded corn,

ripped fully apart
as night unrolled
squirrels and bats with claws of thorn?

I hear a shriek,
fully uncontrolled,
of a settler's wife being scalped and torn.

"Fuck Hate!"

> "What's wrong with assholes, baby? You've got an asshole, I've got an asshole! You go to the store and buy a porterhouse steak, that had an asshole! Assholes cover the earth! In a way trees have assholes but you can't find them, they just drop their leaves. Your asshole, my asshole, the world is full of billions of assholes. The president has an asshole, the carwash boy has an asshole, the judge and the murderer have assholes . . . even the purple stickinpin has an asshole!"
> —Charles Bukowski, *Post Office*

Bukowski dropped his true first name: it reminded him of his father.
He sucked beers in a lost, mournful way and never sought to bother

about his looks but wore short-sleeved buttoned-down shirts, the orts
and sorts of footwear—"post office shoes"—and often baggy shorts.

He was "soft and fat like summer roses," hair short and slicked back,
and his ruined teeth gave him a feral smile that opened like a crack.

The disfiguring acne that covered his face was a pestilence of boils
—"the size of apples," said he—on eyelids, nose, and like gargoyles

appeared even in pustules behind his ears and follicles on his head,
his lips, his tongue, and inside his open mouth to deviously embed.

The poet's way of explaining his face and that raging dermal storm
was (*dixit*) "all my withheld screams, spouting out in another form."

His outsize boozer's nose was bulbous and often running with snot,
below which jutted an outlandish jaw and cold thin lips, always taut,

that matched his sad, slitty eyes that sunk in hollows of greasy skin
sheeted over and mottled with acne scars like the signatures of sin.

He goggled at TV, wrote doggerel, lugged about six-packs of beer,
and referred to his cock as the "purple turnip," never without a leer.

He licked the microphone at readings, devised with a slurping sound,
repeating over and over "Fuck Hate" as if it were a childhood round,

but his major insight was finding assholes in every port of the world,
in poets and paupers, in bottles, babes, in objects furled and unfurled,

and in animals, vegetables, minerals, whatsoever went passing on by,
a cripple's red hand, marching band, what his eye or ear could descry.

Rev. Billy Graham's Presumption

"Amen, I have gotten saved.
Now," stated Billy Graham,
who opposed the depraved
like the patriarch Abraham,

adding lest he be shoddy,
"what now I do can't unsave me—
even if I killed somebody"
—alas, that to me is the key—

I can't ever be unsaved now."
What sort of bollocks is this,
or the faith that would allow
the Lord to go on to dismiss

such flaming presupposition
by a prig splitting such hair!
It seems a holier admission
by far to feel honest despair.

Flower Cookery

Lilac, jasmine, nasturtium, lavender, acacia,
marigolds, violets, hawthorn, rose Eurasia,

apple blossoms, cowslips, lilies, hawthorn,
mallow flowers, peonies, lotus, sloe thorn,

mimosa blossoms, elder flowers, sylvanium,
nosegays, borage, scented-leaved geranium.

Refrain:

*Pulped into pottages, flavorings for soups,
turned into honeys for celebrating groups,*

*baked into custards, brewed as cups of tea,
these flowers are delicious for you and me.*

*Whipped into custards, boiled, batter fried,
pounded with sugar in sweets wet or dried,*

*candied or pickled for use as chutney glaze,
eaten raw in salads, for fritters and soufflés,*

*dissolved into jellies, butters, rich preserves,
hot tarts, mousses, all aspics and conserves.*

Farewell, Kind Friend, and Adieu

I still have to say
as I wandered away
no joy ever increased
nor came down like a feast
as when being away from you.
as when being away from you.
Fol de
Heigh Ho
Fol de
Fol de
Rol
Rol
Fol de Rol

I will add as well
that no living hell
with its red licking flames
could out-bitch the blames
as when being adjacent to you.
as when being adjacent to you.
Fol de
Heigh Ho
Fol de
Fol de
Rol
Rol
Fol de Rol

Slumberers Two (at Four)

Shenandoah likes to sleep
in a sort of kneeling ball
like a worshipper toward Mecca,
(holding a wee piggy to neck her)
something like a double-decker
half genuflection, half sprawl.

Shiloh however prefers
a semi-sidelong crouch,
with piles of animals beside her,
bunny, cow, bat, fox, and spider,
along with a soft plush provider,
a kangaroo with one in pouch.

Shenny drops off on a dime
as if soporifically drugged,
warding off any blanket or puff,
invariably with a firmest rebuff,
and her snores, abrasively rough,
recall a pot being scrubbed.

Shiloh taking ages to zonk
bounces about like a cork,
zealous not to slip out of the world,
flatly insisting her flag be unfurled,
arms wildly waving, legs entwirled,
zapping at maximum torque.

Competing Pedals

It is far easier to speed and be reckless than stop.
Over mastering constraint, we prefer turbo-prop.

What offers the easiest access is what we choose.
We reach for what's nearest and follow all clues.

Haste exceeds caution as right reason we forsake.
Accelerators are located to the right of the brake.

Orange

The Blorenge, located in Wales, more hill than mountain, rhymes with orange if you will take a nominal account in.

A long range in the Atlantic Ocean called Gorringe Ridge can serve the word orange in verse like any fittable bridge.

A sporange is not only a celled sac where spores are made, but it makes as lilting a rhyme as perfect as if it were paid.

On the Occasion of Angela Cormier's Engagement to Be Married

No naiad presiding over streams and brooks
had such alabaster skin and enchanting eyes
as Angela who by any act of glancing looks
startles with the high brightness of the skies,

yet on this special day, as Seth may vouch,
the luster must have been surpassed by joy.
May the blessings of your marriage couch
have such power that nothing can destroy.

May both of you in the marriage you make
find in the vows you state a bond to form,
being loyal to words that you never forsake
whether in sun, rain, darkness, hail, or storm.

Legacy

I want nothing more of the world I know,
—provably, as I course to the end of life—
both of us feeble, old, cold, tired, and sore,

than that oracular rock of myth to bestow
its power through which, fighting strife,
the wind echo-boomed the word *endure*.

Olga Scrapeshave

In the small hours of the morning
when the living rarely see hope

and the dying most likely to die,
sorrow like lead sat on her heart.

Olga looked and could not descry
a single thing that seemed a part

of her life that was not a warning
against any thought to try to cope.

She climbed a high balcony alone
to squint through a dark and mist

as if for a lover or father to see
and then unstrapping her shoes

—she was mad to be free of debris,
of demands, of having to choose—

and stepping into the unknown
she entered the air she kissed.

Trump of Doom

Were the Gospels a failure? Christ himself worried
about the faith that he would find on earth at his Second Coming.
The souls he had touched and drawn to him

seemed isolated in storms unleashed by madmen,
tightening rather than breaking the ever-binding shackles of Satan.
Is not worry the devious enemy of true faith?

Worry, crippling, is cognate to the word to *choke*.
When Christ preached as a child, was he confused by his genius?
Having resorted to parables, did he fear we needed

pictures to learn, highlighted by primary colors,
so that we would worry less about those lessons that invariably
showed us up as idiots, cheapskates, liars?

Mysteries are miracles to the meek and mild,
but when wasn't what is beyond our ken not the occasion of fear?
I tremble at the thundering doomclap in the end

when The Lord himself descends from heaven
with a shout, with the voice of the archangel, and with the trump
of God, when the dead in Christ shall rise first.

Who will not knot his hands and bite his fingers?
Life is all about trouble, bother, distress, upset, agitation and fret,
perturbations, scares, fluster, stress, tax and torment,

choking plagues and brute anxiety, terror, horror,
bedevilment, distress, disquiet, and tension. Waiting *alone* is worry.
Forget the wordy definition of worry—proactive

cognitive risk analysis made to avoid or solve
anticipated potential threats and their potential consequences.
To forfend fear, throw your face on faith.

"I Thirst"

Didn't you, Jesus, fail to conquer thirst
but die with hot vinegar moistening your lips
with dry mad hornets biting your vitals?

No need is deeper or can feel worse
with a sufferer in pain for hallucinating drips
of parched and measureless recitals.

Did you in your mind somehow rehearse
the woman at Jacob's well, her moral slips,
and to just what living water entitles?

Recall even if "water of life" is best,
wouldn't *actual* water slake your tongue's tips
and be so valued as a natural disciple?

I offer water, though in sin submersed,
by quenching my thirst in a holy stewardship
with your love, by drowning all denial.

Was the Hermes Typewriter Made for Rant?

Crankiness is not necessarily apple green,
but notable female grumps—Mary McCarthy, Sylvia Plath,
Jean Rhys, Carson McCullers, among others—

banged out their work, *clanged* out the work,
with rattling non-nonsense on sour non-electric Hermes
the color of bitter pickle, lemon, acid, vinegar,

and the sour grapes of obloquy and envy,
immature and unripe and lime. Can a typewriter convey
splenetic palaver, our imprecating howls?

I call them the Celadons, cracked ceramics
throwing down so much bitchery that, letting it all rip,
the dumb machine oxides green sand metal!

Is spinach hated for naught, crinkled like skin
and not reviled as vegetation for its rumpled sward? Color
dyes us the colors we project, fed up firecats

or fishfaddling female novelists, watergirls
rapping away with loud angry barks for an unkind world,
fingers flailing like *poulpe* or crankly squid,

rap-tapping vert, grass, spinach, verdigris,
and mold on f-f-fapping paper. Hermes was god of thieves,
among the most mischievous of Olympian gods,

a divine trickster. It was a sleek, cool machine,
sporting nicely rounded corners, like intriguing women,
and a lid that snapped down over the keyboard

onto a solid base upon which the typewriter sat,
made perfect for a harridan's walloping spite, hammering,
banging, pounding, thwacking, their lawny rants

rolling over the rock-hard rubber platen like cant.
I see twisted green faces above the clacking box, ramps
for gripes as green as jade makes envy angry.

Annual and Perennial

for William Wordsworth

While nature abides with will benevolent,
no woman I have ever known was faithful,
dedicated with devotional omniprevalent
as pink weigela or white spiraea, tasteful,
loyal in my yard or the peonies in fusion
that burst with perfume blossoms in spring
year after year, joyous beauty in profusion
with grace that yearly fairly seems to sing.
But where in the human world may a heart
be lodged with any permanence, a mainstay
where honest faith or trust rarely plays a part
but behaves solely to deceive and to betray?
Look you to nature's flora solely to secure,
what, perennially you'd have a faith insure.

The Sorrowful Rain of Contrition

It is a rainy November afternoon, and I am sitting
with my lovely girls, age four, who, racing about the rooms,
are all in a dither, enough to make me shout, "Enough,"
not gruffly, I promise, merely for some peace.
They bend to kiss my hands in contrition, and
I am shocked,
truly saddened by the servility,
soft foreheads, hot heads.
When isn't supplication sad?
Are they trying to mimic death? Worried
that they cannot explain sorrow
by any language other than that of pitiable docility?
Fawning from fear?
Aching to be absolved—at four—
by desperation?

Subservience is always terrifying,
forget calling it compliance.
Innocent heads pressed on my heavy hands!
Their heads are *sideways*, to insist on the love they feel,
soft heads, hot foreheads,
pressing for penitence—
Wasn't this the cringing way
servants kissed the Tatar's hands to keep from being caned?
When isn't sorrow supplication?
My heart went frigid inside me at the abject obedience,
the fawning behavior of a slave,
subordinate, hugging the legs of some owner.
I well remember how the terrible rain characterized the day
by the momentous horror of the tears (mine) I felt
as if streaming down a window.

Bad Dream

A sounder of crazed boars
galloped through the midnight I awoke
to find you rattling my door,

standing mad beyond a moor,
your eyes pin-wheeling only to evoke
my death God holds in store.

You Can Virtually Watch a Poppy Bloom

You can virtually watch a poppy bloom
late in sweet May when the sun is high,
blaring straight down a cloudless sky,
its heart in a bulb, the bulb in a plume,

the plume splitting in vegetable steam,
a protuberant swelling, spherule, knob,
rising solid and royal, a queenly orb
just barely open, a vermilion gleam,

its corm, hot globe, swelling and wet,
a rude color agog in an urge to spout,
burgeoning until you just see it sprout,
suddenly the premier garden coquette.

The Anthony ("Antimony") Stibnite Scholarship

Anthony ("Antimony") Stibnite sat up all night, terrified,
chewing his fingernails in the dark by the side of his bed,

worried that the sun is approximately 4.5 billion years old
and that in but five billion years from now, the sun will shed

all of its hydrogen full into helium, and when this occurred
it will transform from the yellow dwarf, now as such dead,

into a red giant, whose diameter will extend well beyond
Venus' orbit, even beyond the orbit of Earth—the dread!—

but in either case, the Earth will be burned into a cinder
and be completely incapable of supporting any life, wed

solely to extinction, in which case we will be barbecued,
of anything real or recognizable not so much as a shred,

and so, what good was it that he was whip kid in science
at Medford High, standing of his class at the very head?

No good! So, Tony downed a bottle of cyanogen chloride
he'd distilled at school, turned sky blue, then cherry red.

A scholarship is given now in his name, his smiling face
on a lovely poster in the lobby, lest anyone be misled.

Wind in a Copper Beech

"I have seen everything except the wind."
—John Keats

While nature abides with will benevolent,
no woman I have ever known was faithful,
dedicated with devotional omniprevalent
as pink weigela or white spiraea, tasteful,
loyal in my yard or the peonies in fusion
that burst with perfume blossoms in spring
year after year, joyous beauty in profusion
with grace that yearly fairly seems to sing.
But where in the human world may a heart
be lodged with any permanence, a mainstay
where honest faith or trust rarely plays a part
but behaves solely to deceive and to betray?
Look you to nature's flora solely to secure,
what, perennially you'd have a faith insure.

Amy Lowell at Night

Amy Lowell could not stand the light of day,
nor could she bear noise or any inconvenience.
Doing things at night was quite the poet's way.
Puffing tiny cigars cut down a bit of vehemence.

At a theater, she would always take a seat
to keep empty those on either side of hers,
and in hotels both adjoining rooms deplete,
so undone was she by anything that stirs.

A hunger for empery kept all the bores away.
No visitor could rudely interrupt at two a.m.
She loved to feel sun-flawed beryl water play
across her naked pounds when bathing them.

At meals she insisted on two plates of soup,
saw lilac May in tall purple ice-cream cones,
and grew soon round as an embroidery hoop,
ham-soft, shiny, and inconsequent of bones.

She baked white cakes, for jujus had a taste.
It has been said that she ate like a macaque.
No coat would quite button across her waist.
She kept her every mirror swathed in black.

Sipping tea in her delicate chinoiserie cups,
she lazed in daybeds, ate Sherry's chocolates,
closing her mind in her dining room deluxe
to people, news, noise, war, and apocalypse.

Hair Is Meant to Hide Behind

"No more hiding behind your hair!" chided the female barber,
a near endocrine dwarf, clapping shut her scissors, snapping

away the cape and brutally neck-dusting poor Dickie Cheddar,
seventy-nine, gone hopelessly bald, with a few last bits of ear-
   shrubbery,

and re-boxing her huge clippers, barked, "No pomade for you,
—no, dammit, no use sweeping over what little's left up there,

like some godforgone fox-pelt. Ain't even enough to blow dry!"
So whenever there is mystery, he wondered, there is roguery?

Snip snip: glittering forfex did its work, stooks of mousy fiber
drifted onto the floor. Something there was she did not know.

Hair is *meant* to hide behind, he thought, and under and below!
Intimacy was the neurosis of solitude for the poor hairless man,

one's locks a camouflage, a disguise, concealment, a sanctuary
for those who secretly wish to keep all the trolls at bay. Clippers

kill us, the snick-snick-snicking scissors sawing away, snatching
the last protection we have to conceal our face the undeserving

have no more right to see than the rude, invasive commands
this diotic midget coiffeuse with her shears demands I hear,

pilling away my curtain. Baldness makes any man defenseless!
Barbershops constitute inquisition. Shove the bump care lotion,

boar brushes, bottles of cologne, powder. My Vitalis is my hair,
or was. Barbers, you hide—crouch behind your swiveling chair.

The Swing

Our two four-year-olds flinging on a hammock
singing as they twirltwist about while swinging,

[kick] *"Fie, fooey, fleece'em, and fly"*

chanting out back and forth, rocking to and fro,
sky to ground, ground to sky, laughing, singing,

[kick] *"Fie, fooey, fleece'em, and fly"*

experience the preternatural rhythm of the push
and pull of this mad world in the act of ringing,

[kick] *"Fie, fooey, fleece'em, and fly"*

body-hurling forward to seize what they want
and wish to grab, snatch, and own by flinging.

Reading *The Lorax*

Beleaguered Samuel Fudge,
reading *The Lorax* to his two toddlers,
understood exactly none of it,

not in that truly important sense
of applying all the seemingly rectifying
twaddle to his own tired life.

Plots of this raddling sort,
born of the chop kind of illogic he hated,
left him only aimless,

while the two little girls,
encouraged by these mystifying hairballs
wheeeee'd-away in song.

Henry Thoreau Fishing

I see Thoreau out on the Aboljacknagesic waters
catching speckled trout and silvery roaches, glistening like jewels.
The primitive rivers in Maine, rudimentary, blue,

had fish "bright fluviatile flowers" of spotted hue,
splashing, rushing to his loud joy, leaping out of the spinning pools,
with the sanctity for him of nature's imprimaturs.

Anthony Bourdain Commits Suicide

"Falsehood is easy, truth so difficult. The pencil is conscious of a delightful facility in drawing a griffin—the longer the claws, the larger the wings, the better, but that marvelous facility which we mistook for genius is apt to forsake us when we wanted to draw a real unexaggerated lion."
—George Eliot, *Adam Bede*

"I was raised without religion. I don't believe in a higher power. I am instinctively hostile to any kind of faith. Certainty is my enemy. You know, I am all about doubt."
—Anthony Bourdain

Anthony Bourdain, the food person, in a hotel room,
no person learned why, decided to take his own life

by hanging himself, according to the French police,
but I'd *always* seen despair in his questioning eyes,

angrified, discontented, all ribbery red, and rubbery
matching his iron-gray hair like twists of shrubbery,

and in any person's cheeks, rutted, lined, stretched,
as if some fiend had taken up a scorper and etched,

—*gravured*—such gulleys, are mainly lines of grief,
matched as well by a look so bugged at and put-upon,

that even a proficient wise-ass is capable of despair,
the anguish in success where distress does not abate.

When he laughed that joyless laugh of his, iron tight,
you could almost see him cry, his face as hard as slate.

He was no great chef, yet claimed to be, washed pots,
began as a lowly *plongeur* in a dive in Provincetown,

but saw that a warmouth gets attention by noisy ploys,
which became fun for him, a way of excreting drugs.

I felt I also saw a gawky tallness worked against him,
with him in sitting never quite sure where to put his legs.

He had a magenta face, facing away from a real face,
anxious, perturbed, uneasy, fearful, and overwrought,

jumpy, dubious, rattled, het up, edgy, antsy, strung out,
in a stew, all of it keyed into a sarcasm, apprehensively

admitting *I don't like me because I'm a squirrelly fake.*
Suicides, by the way, very much want you to go away.

Get off my back, you TV slackers! Fuck off, drones!
Don't you see anyone at all can like or not like food?

Opinions come with these noodles and are as glassy,
my attitudes are easy as shrugs and only shame me!

It is said *one's life is rounded with the same few facts,*
the same simple relations everywhere, and it is vain

to travel to find it new: that is what touring revealed
to him, confirming, disclosing, his dark emptiness,

for he always brought himself along to where he was,
whether to Bangkok, Glasgow, Beirut, Tokyo or Laos.

Racing brings us to a rest we inevitably co-opt. Travel
inevitably takes you, to where you have to be stopped.

Opening an Envelope Begins a Pavane

Opening an envelope begins a pavane.
The thick ivory paper crackles in protest to being unfolded,
but relents in smoothing out like rest,

at least with creamy vellum or pale bond
which never spreads out with any sense of stretch but eases
to a proportion fit to the caressing hand,

yielding to suitable angles shaped to be read,
the paper folds as sedate and formal as rooms in a vicarage
allowing invited guests a formal entrance.

Sleeve and casing, swaddle and swathed,
there is a grace in the intricate way, a tiny dancing comfort,
a letter comes in its silvery clothing to you.

Why Do Fat Italian Guys with Flourishes

Why do fat Italian guys with flourishes,
showily dumping red canned tomatoes into pots
yammering on about adding sausages,

basil, oil, yellow onions, a bit of sugar—
Frank Sinatra loved to claim his sauce was perfect—
always adding some secret cockamamie

ingredient like a piece of pork or veal,
make such a big noise over a nothing preparation?
They appear in lots of gangster movies,

crowing about their rare culinary gifts,
sweatily stirring the sauce while munching bread.
"Pepperoncini for some zing—*assoluto!* —

then sliced garlic in the 'gravy,' *capisce?*
[They do not know the term for "gravy" in Italian,
who may say *sugo* or *ragu*] and budda bing!"

Any silly towhee with its *zweek zeek zeek*
sitting on a tree branch and stretching its little neck
makes far more effort with its song, and is

not only never spattered with red sauce
or seasonings, but isn't wearing a wife beater's T-shirt
and fist-squeezing a ripped-off hank of bread.

The Roundness of Emily Dickinson

Emily spent more than forty long years
in her circular bedroom, on the second floor. Circumferences
primly dominated her small vocabulary,

and she applied the word assiduously.
She called the hallway, darkly seen opening the front door,
the "Northwest Passage," because it had

six exits, small spokes, as it were, to dodge
away from any visitors. Her very concept of communion,
however, was quite as round as her clocks,

"Calvinist clocks" that tolled the hours
in round numbers of the world around her. Impregnable
of eyes, she scoped all she wished to see.

and no more. The act of looking is itself
is round, when looking around taking everything in,
including sunsets, sunrises, the whorls

of worlds. To reduce the facts of life, in fact
is to round them likes the pies she always loved to bake
in solitary communion with herself,

crimped, in her bedroom, ever ready when
downstairs, owlish, in the hall through any exit to bolt
circumferentially to not be seen, if spied.

Henry Thoreau Sleeping Under a Board

> "Those who have never tried it can have no idea how far a door, which keeps the single blanket down, may go toward making one comfortable."
> —*A Week on the Concord and Merrimack Rivers*

Henry Thoreau, having walked to
high cloudy Hoosack mountain, outside
slept nightly under an old deal door,

after digging a well with his hands
and a sharp stone—he had also gobbled
water from holes in a horse's tracks—

boiling his favorite supper of rice,
slurped up with a whittled wooden spoon
over a fire made with found scraps

of old newspapers that he took time
to read for rustic entertainment, amused
by old adverts from Boston firms,

and then under a moon like a pasha,
in pillows, he encased himself in boards,
doors he in dreams he stepped through.

"Sympathetic Interviews"

Childless, vain, multi-divorced movie or TV stars
love being interviewed in *Vogue* and *Vanity Fair* but create the
  question mark
above their empty uteruses, ironically *encouraging*

talk about frigidity, baby-shaming, split-blaming,
and the perception that non-mothers are "damaged goods,"
  pathetically hinting
that not finally becoming a mother was not planned,

the torrent of any nosy interviewer's rude intrusions
feeding the vanity of the illogical nest-empty that she hopes is
  winning her pity
despite that she's still running around trying to find a seat,

keep a husband, have a baby, rock a bassinet, yet *still*
the motherless no-go by blabbing away, hoping to appear sensitive
  and worthy,
is reminding everyone she has no husband and even worse

is still a childless failure, so questions about her never end,
wherever the interview goes. My sage advice? Why don't you just
  stifle?
Cut the cackle. Button it. Impound. Shut your pie hole!

There are no sympathetic interviews. Sensitive, cruel, sisterly,
thoughtful—whatever the nature of the approach—it all serves to
  reinforce
you, unproven, fishy, excusive, are still not a woman.

Sapling Oak

The trunk of an oak sapling is celandine
with light mottled spots freckled by sun

that in summer heat fade to a gentle dun
as if to balance for style the yellow green,

and the natural hues of its silken strength
give a wave of promise in that chartreuse

of mineral joy to tiny leaves of like hues
and for all its youth endow it with length

that truly seem when light breezes blow
to stretch itself out in a tall slender reach

as a young flirt might the world beseech
to bless her new green frock of pistachio.

Go Anywhere But Back

Walking responds to any prompt of zeal
and even getting lost on a specific track,

becomes a boon of fiction over fact,
a blessing of what nature would reveal

to you, resolved to think instead of feel,
posing questions of the tight, the slack,

challenging us by what we fear we lack
in matters, say, that we wish to conceal.

Know the strongest defense is to attack.
For the timid the unknown is never real.

Fortitude, of all the many ways to heal,
divides the brave from the running pack.

Say yes to every walk whatever the tack,
Take a chance. Manufacture no appeal.

Wherever your walk may lead is the ideal.
Turn left or right. Go anywhere but back.

Early Meadow Rue

for Nanda Devi Unsoeld

I offer you blade, stipule, and petiole
of its shady leaf blade,

raised, awl-shaped, at your high soul,
my lifelong renegade,

and ask you to take it to dusky Sheol
where you'll be weighed,

to flower again on a Himalayan knoll
when I'll appear in a glade

to read on the bloom a prophetic scroll,
grateful fate has been paid.

Death Is the True Beginning of Real Life

Death is the true beginning of real life
transporting all creatures to eternity
beyond all facts of trouble and strife
with a farewell to earthly maternity.

Fear has projected a curtain of black,
where weaklings squat in uncertainly,
and habit reminds us of all we lack
with repeating masks of modernity.

Shed the years you have been given
and the fatuous front of fraternity
Of cruel apprehension feel shriven
to embrace, at last, lasting serenity.

Authorize Appropriately

A serious gardener should always be a scold,
hating weeds with a scorn she holds for men,

tearing at their heads with any snapping tool,
muddy-kneed and vile as any scratching hen.

A bitch flinging orts is at home in the tares,
slashing venomous mad in stubbles of dirt.

The perfect cropper is someone who pares
beds of orts and thrills at living things hurt.

Song for Shiloh and Shenandoah

Bring no sadness to your sweet dreams
Sing out for gladness in blue extremes
Know I'll be true
whatever you do
in the velvet quiet of night
through dark and the light
when things don't go right

Refrain:
It takes more muscles to frown
much more than ever to smile
Whatever, please never stay down
And all will come right in awhile

Fatal Gift

Azalea leaves and their nectar
are poisonous, the mere haze

of which, a floating perfume,
can come over you in a daze.

its glib flowers a death threat
if handed you in a black vase.

Henry Thoreau the Walker

> "True and sincere traveling is no pastime, but it is as serious as the grave. . . . I do not speak of those that travel sitting, the sedentary travelers whose legs hang dangling the while, mere idle symbols of the fact, any more than when we speak of sitting hens we mean those that sit standing, but I mean those to whom traveling is life for the legs, and death too, at last. The traveler must be born again on the road, and earn a passport from the elements, the principal powers that be for him."
> —*A Week on the Concord and Merrimack Rivers*

Henry, a jack-of-all-trades, was ever a real wonder walking.
He had a tin cup strapped to a belt, with a saucepan on his back

and on all ramblings carried a dipper, a big spoon, fishing line,
Indian meal, salt, and sugar. He'd habitually buy bread en route

at fourpence a loaf. Traveling for him was never riding trains,
like some flannel-mouthed loafer with soft limousine feet up,

fobbing off with pretense he is Fremont or Bridger facing trials.
He beat through the thorny woods with unbent trousers of duck

or kerseymere or corduroy, wore a furry hat, serviceable shoes,
a thick pepper-and-salt waistcoat. He *repaired* through forests!

A stranger seeing him fix one, thought him an umbrella-mender.
(Henry often carried a brolly abroad, even when the sun shone.)

Perambulating taught him ingenuity. He was known in Concord
for his handy manner, fixing old clocks, surveying, horseshoeing,

haying, but it was his oaken legs he worked as hard as his mind
in forests, in the elements, hard rain, blowing snow, windblown,

just the sort of weather all of the dilettante amateur Holofernes
wordy, peering through train windows, are glad they are out of!

Grandfather Herod, Son, and Grandson

Antipater the Idumaean
brought up a family and sought
by power to build them.

Herod the Great, hateful,
and one of his two sons, sought
to murder all the children.

His son Antipas captured
Johannes the Baptist and sought
his head and killed him.

They excoriated Christ
and to cause his death they sought
but never stilled him.

Castaway

A Jew cannot eat a pelican.
Mr. Gabbai who was starving on the island
inquired of his empty soul

upon having been left marooned
when there was so little fresh water or food,
why this bird with its dumb gape,

gobbling blue fish, draining water
from its long scooping beak, was considered
detestable *sheketz, kaloshesdik,*

shteyndidik by strict Levitical fiat, so
disgusting, filthy? He squinted at its smug pouch
filled with gannets, its billowing belly,

and grizzled: *it wasn't a rock badger!*
It had no fins, no scales, no big cloven hooves—
the meeskait thing just perched there!

The old cocker had wandered bleakly
along the tightening coast in flapping rubber shoes,
in wet Peru, where the tourist boat

had left him after he had disembarked
to photograph some clouds and entered a cave to pee,
and now he pondered his missing stools,

why should he be hollow, empty, bare,
void of matter? He eyed the pelican. Could nothing
be done to make this clacker kosher?

Why are mere ducks or goose allowed us?
he moaned. Wouldn't his butcher, bald Mr. Kriah
from Merrick, New York, salt it for him with

no fanfare? He was ravenous! He'd eat him!
What is *bitldik* about some odd shoe-billed clownbird,
ekidik in some tall, ugly, strutting foygi,

all beak and mailbox mouth? "Screw dietary laws!"
howled Mr. Heshy Gabbai, racing to build a driftwood fire
of his underwear, running up and down the beach,

bald as a spoonbill, a crazy Long Island Jew
tripping and stoning the bird and cooking it and biting
through the feathers, whereupon it thundered

rain over remote Ballestas, hammering hard
under the blackened sky with one crazed lightning bolt
striking the poor starving *yutz stone dead!*

Phillips Andover Faculty

> "Such treatment I did not expect, for I never had a patron before. . . . Is not a patron, my lord, one who looks with unconcern on a man struggling for life in the water, and when he has reached ground, encumbers him with help?"
> —Dr. Johnson to Lord Chesterfield

A sett of badger, fortress of mole,
a drey of squirrel, a holt of otter,
inch-small each, weak as water,
scurrying hot for the safety hole,

remind me of you and your coven
of gossips, the treason of groups,
calumnies ruling insidious troops,
fearing light of truths to govern.

An aggregation of fat manatee,
skulk of foxes, murder of crows,
But no, *never* a crash of rhinos,
no—bigness you could never be.

God Is Being

God is Being, fully in act:
"I am that I am," truly.

Isness is never potency.
but fills out action, duly.

Lord means "he lets be,"
quite literally and truly.

He is achieved in total,
realized and ever newly.

He is never Becoming,
but awake, alive, fully.

God alone is total act,
utterly and acutely.

"Before Abraham was, I am,"
said Jesus absolutely.

Glacier Ice

Where sea meets ice, the water shimmers crystal,
washed peaks splashing peacock blue. Just below

the surface, ice forms bands of aqua and turquoise,
bird's egg blue, as colors different shapes bestow,

then indigo that becomes a kind of cobalt, a steel
or midnight Prussian frowning with a lesser glow,

nothing now of teal, but a beetling delft, darkly
changing to a brooding storm-cloud blue, now,

bleaker than draconian slate like a dungeon tomb,
to a sunless depth that only the blind alone know.

The Final U-Turn of Clara Bay Fingerhood

Buying her necessities at the Giant Eagle, kept waiting in line
at the check-out always infuriated Miss Clara Bay Fingerhood,

irked at the influx of new tourists every Memorial Day, fat, rich,
New Yorkers, New Jersey people, loud renters who overbought

groceries in great walloping carts, purchased liquor by the case,
and parked anywhichway in town, as if they *owned* Cape Cod!

Now Miss Clara Bay was on the front grass of her old fort house,
angrily waving away the automobile moving in her driveway,

howling out at rather than speaking to the motorist *"Dammit
don't you see the sign?"* Wearing her ratty Welsh plain robe

she gave it to the driver with the bark off, for people—tourists,
wash-a-shores—just went right ahead turning on her property

for donkey's years, where in Wellfleet the dead-end, perfectly
stated with a sign, met the Old Polpis Road that led onto Route 6A.

So why did all these jackasses always keep nosing into her land,
as if it were theirs? "'No U-Turns'! There it reads in bold letters,

which means you and you and you!" The mad old maid got little
in the way of town assistance, paying outrageous property taxes

when she had no mail delivery, no trash pick-up, never a single
child in school, no snowplow for her road in the dead of winter,

no benefits, no man about. "*Get out!*" she spat out the window
one August night, spying at the dune-end of her road an old car

just about to back into her driveway when running out directly
into its blinding head lights, it swerved and instantly killed her.

"I sold her the very push broom she was apparently wagging
when she went down," said Mr. O. P. Pine at the Giant Eagle,

its cashier, "and, dang it, wasn't it only yesterday Clara went
butting in line and I had to tell the ol' gal, 'It's not your turn'?"

The Cycle of Willamette Sours

Antique shops kept her stones under lock
and key, "Oh, you sell Willamette Sours!" visitors
cried, browsing shops in Commercial Street,

knowingly repeating in sing song, "'The point
of the sea is to see.' Remember?" There were books
about her and her suicide drowning years ago.

Her artistic stones she lovingly collected
not on the ocean side, but in the circular bay, where,
embraced, she said, "All's loved by a circle."

Willamette Sours walked the dunes daily
the many years she lived in Provincetown, discovering
stones that she could write on, tiny slogans

that came to her like the cold, salty breezes
off Race Point. She had never married, had been born
in Arkansas in 1931, and a love of landscape,

after a bout of polio, sent her to art school,
where designs in all of her insistently oval paintings
revealed, not so much a lack of originality

or boldness as a penchant for lesbianism
that her parents, shocked, could not countenance.
A spell living alone in New York City alone

forced her to ask deep questions of herself
that she knew by the clarity of her inability to answer
could only be revealed by avoiding,

not repeating. "It was Ruskin who declared,"
she explained to visitors, drinking at the Lobster Claw,
handing out her stones, cylindrical, rounded,

bulbous, fat with force, inscribed with slogans,
vulva-like in their messages, meanings soft, vatic, cool,
truly prescient and, in a real sense, holy,

"to see clearly is poetry, prophecy, and
religion—all at once," and so even into her late eighties
it was the lucidity, coherence, and dedication

of her trudges in the sand for finding stones
to decorate that became her lonely faith. It was the sea,
the dark green sea, that not only threw them up

to paint and adorn but willingly, wildly, absorbed
those hard questions in her life that she had relinquished.
The Lobster Claw keeps a semi-circular shelf

of her stones to this day, a bow-shaped sphere
with its array of discoids, hoop-shaped, round, globoidal
ring-stones with saws. "The point of the sea

is to see," she had scribbled in one final note
that she had left on her davenport last March before loading
her pockets with some, to enter the waves.

The Black Grapes of Calcatoggio

There seemed to be witch face in every grape.
The Corsican noir I tasted, Sciacorello with its berry skin,
had been insinuated into a very strange varietal

vitis vinifera, black grapes made red now dark.
What I believed to be a parent vine of the Ligurian-Tuscan
wine grape, *pollera nera*, went oddly unblended,

and the temptress who served me in Calcatoggio,
spread her hand on mine with a mountain glint in her eye
under a fishlight sky. Music was playing inside,

and the grapes from the bowl I was sampling, all
of them globed, came thrums. "*Voli ballà?*" she asked me,
but I couldn't dance, heady from the perfume,

secreted in the grapes and wine, she solicitously
fed me. Few understood their wines, the beauty explained,
and I agreed, for mine, a facsimile of mammolo,

I felt, was not exported, like many, why I never knew,
not then, and not the following week that I spent with her,
overlooking a plage I had not recalled ever seeing,

the face of a stupefying mountain in the distance,
glimpsed from an empty bed and a just as empty window,
at dawn, waking with no memory, fully expressed.

Shiloh and Shenandoah and The Doors

> "Break on through to the other side
> Break on through to the other side
> Yeah, yeah, yeah, yeah."
> —The Doors

At five years old, they *heed* Jim Morrison!
The organ glissades of "Love Me Two Times,"
send my poppets into jumping transports,

a true Dionysian frenzy, as they sway
to the extra-frenetic *squirrely* driving, drumbeat
like little hippified demons, true believers

in rebellion, waving their hands as if
"*Ah yes!*" sitting up front at the Whisky a Go Go
and not confined to car seats, belted

with straps instead of ice-cold beers.
"*Play that again, Daddy,*" howls yipping Shiloh,
Shenandoah adding, "*I love thumps!*"

That "People Are Strange" they believe
already, but the insistence of that *baaad* guitar?
They buy it with pop-eyed conviction.

"Roadhouse Blues," "L.A. Woman,"
"Riders on the Storm" evoke wild organ shrieks
and no end of with-it head bobbing.

What have I done to my sweet girls
but turned them both into raving, psychedelic geeks
for wild rockers and heart-throbbing?

No Bird in the Hand, No Bush

A zero-sum game
is oddly the same
as a zero-sum gain
and so makes sense
as to dollars and cents
the go and the come
since a zero-sum game
results it is plain
in a gain of a sum
of absolute zero
regarding expense
with zero to claim
and none to blame
as to feeling shame
about anyone's aim
since it has no hero.

Verecundia, the Punishment Whore

"She's like you!" snarls the intemperate scold,
out of control, jelly-brained, demanding fealty

of a two-year-old, classically favoring one twin
over another by leaving the one behind. This is

truly from bad fairy-tale legend. I cringe to see
your barking fire-self again let loose, on display

for one tiny little soul to suffer and yet another
witness, but what both of them will remember

is how in crime little children never have a say,
which fits to a T the guileful way of any shrew.

You should be ashamed of yourself, of course,
but then you would be someone else, not you.

Henry Thoreau and His Lichen Repasts

A bit of nose he had on him,
sniffing at the bark of twigs,
sitting alone in forest glades
listening to the brittlecreak
of tall hardwoods in the fall
and, chewy as good wet figs,

sampling the tangy tastes
of lichen like a nosing moose,
especially black stone flower
and tiny fans of rock tripe—
umbilicaria—with pine nuts
he efficiently put to use

by brewing hot bracing teas,
squatting like a *coureur de bois*.
He enjoyed reindeer lichen,
cold-hardy, by taking it dry,
crushing and then boiling it,
like leaves of Ceylon regular,

soaking it in water until soft.
eating it mixed with berries,
fish eggs, or lard. He used it
also as diarrhea cure for lichen
gas, blessing its red juice and
the many ways Nature varies!

Christ's Lineage Included Women Prostitutes

Is it any wonder Jesus was gentle to tarts?
Rahab, an ancestor of his by family charts
is lauded as an example of living by faith,
although a whore she played nothing safe,
for she strolled the city a repulsive wraith,
immune to cruel jibes and society's darts.

According to Matthew's scripture report
Tamar was an ancestor of Jesus, in short.
And by his father Judah, their son, Perez,
ancestor to King David, so Genesis says,
so, through a harlot's line that son of his,
is related to Christ by that venal disport.

Ruth of Moab, great-grandmother of David,
was also a part of Christ's lineage, shaded
by Boaz by sleeping, a Gentile, at his feet
to ensnare the man by a plan so complete
that when he awoke he knew love's defeat,
immune as he was to the wiles of the jaded.

The right of Jesus to the Davidic throne
was by way of Solomon, for it is shown
how *Bathsheba*, Uriah's *and* David's wife,
an interplay lusty with full guile and strife,
seduced Judah's king in a land fully rife
with lust, but honor and chastity flown.

Appeasing Hannah Screecham

When any customer barked a shin on his oyster boxes
or stumbled over the clam rakes, scoopers, or grapples

cluttering—"foozling up," as he put it—the wet rooms
of his oyster shanty perched at the edge of Sandy Neck,

old Zekariah Tattersall kicked gloves and rubber boots
away to say, "We need a blow to clean this place out!"

Wise in the ways of water and wind, before any storm
he would remove small items, nail down larger ones,

and open windows and doors, leaving fierce hurricanes
a way to blow through. "If a problem cannot be solved,

enlarge it," he'd say with an avizeful eye, removing
his pipe, and then look way, convinced by long habit

no one would believe it. "The eyes are not responsible,
when the mind does the seeing," he'd say, folding rope

or boxing his Wellfleets. But it worked for old Zeke
in every bad nor'easter, blowing gale, or violent storm

for other shanties that had been boarded up collapsed
in sticks or floated away. "Want to know what I say?"

he'd ask with a grin. "Appease Hannah Skreecham!"
By her he meant the old New England mythic witch,

an old outcast harridan who, feared by every child,
was accused of witchcraft and hanged without a trial.

One never was quite sure by what he said, whether
she was to blame for the implacable winds of force

he fought by his wily accommodating Yankee wit
or the cause of the messes underfoot he'd mutter at.

Nightmare

for R. L. Stevenson

At the River Ness and Moray Firth,
by name in eeriness both give birth

to scary dreams I carry throughout
of direst poverty, of living without

as a pilgrim plodding over the earth,
empty of purse and deleted of worth,

facing a darkness as loud as a shout,
with nothing to do but wander about,

finding no exit, of food but a dearth,
night demons all a-gibber with mirth,

for this weird estuary forms a snout
of a bizarre creature ready to spout

venom, its trunk of a sinister girth
born in a darkness all facing north.

I strive to awake with fist and clout,
but chimera here allows no one out.

At the River Ness and Moray Firth,
by name in eeriness both give birth

to scary dreams I carry throughout
of direst poverty, of living without.

Winifred Pineweevil Who Never Shuts Up Talks All the Time

Winnie Pineweevil, who never shuts up, talks all the time
in detailed reports of all her intentions speaking to empty air,
feels, in her harebrained life, it crucially important to share
what she is doing or planning to do with reason and rhyme
thrown open to the wind, for prattling on is solely her point,
chuntering on about weather, headaches, or shopping lists
basically, everything of what in her irrelevant life consists,
droning on and on just how her groinball went out of joint,
a prattle, a babble, a chatter, a gabble like amassing vapor
infusing a room to produce in everyone migraines that kill,
incessant sound like a *screee* of a dentist's murderous drill
with a high shrillness that can turn a mind as pale as paper.
If Beethoven Winnie's husband had been, pondering a clef,
he would have thanked the Almighty for making him deaf.

Cider Apples

Hangdown, Chibble's Wilding, Kentish Fill-Basket, and Glory of
　　the West
are cider apples, you can tell by the juicy resonances that promise a
　　biting snap.

A drink made from crushing anything shows a mastery, but with
　　fruit a promise
must be made to be manly, as well, which is why the word *pressing*
　　best applies

and farmers in New Hampshire who, loving the wild, scratted down
　　crabapples
from their bold angry orchards until the musty juice squeezing from
　　the pomace

flowed like gold, not perry or cyder but hardy replicas of what the
　　Pilgrims drank,
apples with high levels of acid & tannin, sugar sharp bitter spitters
　　for fermenting

into tart drinks. Brown Snouts, Chisel Jerseys, Newtown Pippins,
　　Black Dabinetts
come from trees highly resistant to apple scab, canker, and fire
　　blight. And why?

Cider apples contain a lot of tannin that, like rugged men, snapping
　　crisp wrists,
produce a distinctive, bitter flavor in their fruit. No, give me tough
　　red Foxwhelp,

hard as horn, for my tankard, not the prim, sweet garden apples
　　Aunts Mildred,
Edna, and Beryl used to concoct sissy pies for Mothering Sunday. I
　　want tang!

Matthew 24:42–44

There was no moon, no wind, no swell,
the night *Titanic* went rushing through the sea,
an absolute calm of a truly unusual kind,

when not even an ocean mist could blind,
conditions for sighting an iceberg to any degree
unlikely. The absence of swell or waves

meant, as well, no ring of surf would appear
around the waterline of any berg in an ocean lea,
nor was white moonlight seen to reflect it.

The iceberg lacked any crystalline quality
to give it a shape of visibility, except as absentee,
just as in curling one sweeps to straighten

the ship as it sailed seemed sure in the calm
a terrible repose that with undeviating certainty
indicated that nothing unshapen could harm.

It is the *unlikely* moment, we're told, when
death like a thief in the night by fateful decree
collects us, to disappear, without an amen.

Jesus in Bethany

The irony of death and life
is that they stare at each other so!
If Jesus had been willing to stay
out of Judea, he would have avoided
the cruel actions of the Sanhedrin.
What brought him back was
the death of Lazarus,
his friend, who lived in Bethany,
a town about two miles east of Jerusalem,
which for any Galilean,
unloved there, was hazardous
and never a region for clemency,

so, when Jesus' disciples failed
in their efforts to persuade him
not to return to Judea, the chief priests
immediately took black counsel together
at the news of Jesus appearance,
and from that day forth sought
to put the man to death. Their avarice,
and a forked sense of enmity
(the accent alone they loathed)
for a notorious Galilean,
although Lazarus rose rapturous
as life conquered death to revelry.

Rosa on a Bicycle

According to Rosa Luxemburg, Marx had erred in his *Capital* in that the proletariat could not *afford* to buy the commodities

it produced, and therefore by his own criteria it was impossible for any capitalists to make a profit in a closed-capitalist system,

since the demand for commodities would be too low, therefore many commodity values could not be transformed into money.

Capitalists in consequence (said Rosa) sought to realize profits by offloading extra commodities onto non-capitalist economies,

hence the phenomenon of imperialism, as capitalist states seek to dominate weak economies, all of it leading to the destruction

of non-capitalist economies, as they are increasingly absorbed into a capitalist system. With death to non-capitalist economies

however, there would be no more available markets to offload surplus commodities onto, and capitalism would break down.

The limits of the capitalist system must drive it to imperialism, therefore, thus I offer you a version of Rosa's cyclic surrealism.

Fritz Haber Invented Poison Gas

Fritz Haber invented poison gas,
writing down "C x t = k."
In World War I, it suffocated *en masse*
gasping soldiers like breathing cut glass.
A German Jew devised this spray:
the lethal gas, note, was Zyklon B.
whereon the Nazis without any delay
but with hideous ironic glee
used it on his own race, perfect prey.

Jump Rope Song

Sharp pieces of glass do best to scrape down to pare
axe helves, rake stales, flail staves, all wooden ware.

Tell us whom you love to hate to say a quick prayer.
Axe helves, rake stales, flail staves, all wooden ware.

Scrape away,
scrape away,
scrape way, mister.
Any sharp tool
will kill your sister.

The Village Store,
Mr. Woodshake, Prop.

I.

Nobody knew his first name.
He wore heavy flannel shirts,
smoked Edgeworth tobacco, saved screws,
and cut nails in the old blue cans that he would never discard.
He had kept the store in Sippewisset for donkey's years.
His sister, Mercy, put food by
in Mason jars, pickalillies and pickles,
and he sold little packets of spruce gum.
He had a distaste for hand shaking,
declaring, "It is a hollow useless ceremony
and wastes my time. Wishing isn't doing. Nope.
Time is my price—
I set it by the stack.
Money is flat and meant to be piled."

II.

Typically, adjusting his specs,
he tallied up your purchases with chalk
on a chalkboard. An old coffee grinder
stood on the counter. On the wooden shelves stood jars of candy
(caramel balls, Mary Janes, bolster bars, nigger toes, etc.),
badger shaving brushes,
jars of maple syrup, crackers, darning eggs,
handmade soaps, corncob dolls, stove blacking,
wool hats, rubber wading boots,
fishing poles and wheels of cheddar cheese
that he cut and quickly wrapped.
"Good cheese must be sharp," he told customers,

never directly looking at them,
lecturing them mainly by way of mutters.

III.

He was flinty—a tightwad.
He almost always ate a raw turnip for lunch,
taking a knife to slice off the purple top
and carefully scrape round the insides for pulp he could eat.
He sold root beer, horn combs, gloves, pestles,
grafting wax, jars of honey, unguents and salves,
shingle frows, lard, even house-framing
plans he personally drew up. "You can't build
a log cabin out of hemlock with bark on it," he'd say,
"or it'll rot in a couple of seasons. Well-plans
I've thrown in for digging. Twenty-five feet is a good well."
He made his own ink, burning a fat pine knot,
hold it under a piece of metal, then collect the smoke,
then scrape the lampblack off into a can.

IV.

No store item was ever marked down.
Whenever a customer pontificated
about maple sugar grades, for everyone
somehow was expert on them—pale colors were the best
—or set a can back on the shelf
assbackwards, it tended gravely to upset him.
He would adjust his spectacles and say,
"Don't ever take a fence down
until you know why it was put up."
His sister taught children
in a one-room schoolhouse
where at lunch, cooked on an old cast-iron
Glenwood wood-burning stove with two burners,
she served salmon pea-wiggle.

V.

"You want moah?"
whenever you shook a bag, dubiously,
gauging its weight.
His nose was long and sharp and pink,
like a Yankee weathervane. But he was sharp at everything,
like tearing off paper from a white roll
for wrapping up packages,
using the "store-keeper's knot"—
a one-handed move, using forefinger and thumb
and then, with a looping-wrap of the string
around his left forefinger
he'd snap the string, so it cut itself, sharply!
There was an edge to whatever he said, "Careful,"
he'd murmur, "That knife is aciculated."

VI.

"No, no winter apples," he'd squawk, "we pick 'em
just before the first good frost when they're just hard enough
To withstand thumb pressure!"
"I need that dough knife atop there,"
he fussed, with a grabber tool, a reach stuck,
stepping over the wash sticks, spiles, sap pails
wooden rakes, hay forks, barrels of tree nails,
apple butter paddles, apple sleds, splint baskets,
burl mallets, rows of horn books,
one-piece hickory twig brooms, sap funnels,
Wash tubs, eel traps, sap spoons, button-hole hoops,
pie crimpers, piggins, apple peels,
wooden meat pounders, rundlets.
"You wanna have it wrapped up to go?"

VII.

He fed logs to the stove
in winter. There were oyster crackers,
pie tins, wooden spatulas, and nails
sold from pull out drawers. He sold apple presses, door stones
flour scoops, gentian, cider, stove mitts,
wooden toys, lamps, porcelain chamber pots, neck yokes,
and pairs of cotton work gloves. Canning jars,
gardening supplies, and all sorts of sewing notions
also rested on many of the shelves.
There were tapping irons, and steel spouts for sugaring.
"For a good sap day there must be a west wind
and bright sunshine," he said. "The cold sap is the best quality; when
there's an icicle or even a trace of one on the spout
you know you've got it."

VIII.

Outside he kept roof slate, fence posts,
post-hole diggers, burlap-balled trees saplings,
rakes, a pile of tanned cow hides, and scythes,
shovels, mauls, auger, buck saws, scoring axes, spokeshaves,
snaths, "The only one kind of snath—scythe handle—
you can get nowadays, is ash,"
he lamented, "bent around jigs in a factory. We always used
a steam-bent, black cherry snath growing up,
no pussyfooting," he said and spat at a pot.
He would gesture with his pipe, saying,
"Nope. You can't find a good snath anymore,"
You stood outdoors with him, cold, always a bit
anxious, fearing his temper.
Going outside, he expected you to buy!

IX.

He kept snug over his ear a pencil,
which he shaved to sharpen. He honed-in on
whatever he did. He sold rows of jams, flails, needles,
swingles and staves, both. Baskets of garlic and eye potatoes
sat on the floor in spring, and bottles of
strong sap beer ("I don't believe that man ever lived
that could drink two eight-ounce glasses
and walk ten minutes later," he would declare.)
Customers didn't leave but stood about talking near his stove.
"Small towns make up for their lack of people,"
he often grizzled, "by having everyone being nosy."
Whenever he bumped into you in mid aisle,
he would repeatedly mutter,
"Clear a way, Granny Haddock!"

Handsome Dan

The Yale bulldog's traditional name
recalls for me in terms of looks just
how our department secretaries must
without a stretch identify with same.

They slaver, grump, and all appear
muscular and hefty, their loose hose
wrinkled as their faces, with a nose
on each pushed in, rough short hair

that fits with hanging skin, underbite,
upturned jaw prognathic, jutting teeth,
legs bent, bowed, their bums beneath,
their frown a rope-fold of pure spite,

bulging out eyes like a yellow loquat.
Comparing both, muzzle to muzzle?
I'll confess I find nothing to puzzle.
Between them give me the mascot.

St. Joan of Arc's Feast Day, May 30, Paris

St. Joan of Arc's ashes were thrown into the Seine in 1431, where I paused more than five hundred years later to pray to her spirit to watch over me as I knelt by the river to say thanks to her, that night, that the day of my life had begun.

Yahweh's Covenant with Israel

How could any normal god command
utter extermination of the Amalekites,

the Hebrews savaging them like kites,
killing women and children in hand?

Yahweh, a big gerrymandering god,
loved (as we read) to redistrict land

according to his whim and planned
to drive away any he found a fraud,

and so with fancy and utter caprice
allowed the Jews (or so they boast),

serving the while their private host,
an entire nation and let them fleece

the true owners and dwellers there
and gave them as if drawing a line

their irredentist claim to Palestine
without a mortgage, free and clear,

and just as freely chose to obliterate
by quirk all the Hivites, Canaanites,

and peaceful, land-owning Hittites
just to hand over Israel real estate,

driving all owners out of their huts,
frightened and disenfranchised now,

no hearth to have, no land to plough
to suffer in exile as disordered mutts,

which serves to prove divine vitriol,
is a rat's nest of bias and prejudice,

evicting natives in acts venomous
to reward—arbitrarily!—Israel.

Henry Thoreau Loved Common Weeds

Henry Thoreau who loved common weeds
hoed out with grunts by millions of farmers aiming
to clear the land, treasured their beauty

and found their appetite to live brave and bold
and radical, not the groveling exclamations of horror
all the hoeing Cushes, Nimrods, and Shaphats

in overalls, with their greedy furrow-fucking
dreams for money, zipping off their stalks and heads,
hated and sought to ridicule with low names

like pigweed. lousewort, chickweed, red root,
henbit, deadnettle, black medic, red root, nutsedge,
stinging nettle, common couch, finger grass,

fire tree, bindweed, crabgrass, quackgrass,
creeping charlie. Why, a weed, determined Henry,
is but a plant growing where not wanted,

filled with seeds, loathed because abundant,
hated because vigorous, despised because fecund,
emerging triumphant over all lands, lanes,

pastures, such is their pluck and vigor.
Henry for whom weeds lighted up like joggle sticks
cooked them, ate them, drank them in tea,

applied them on wounds, used them in salads,
and gave them lovely names like amaranth, ambrosia
mistflower, fairy crassula, white bryony.

What you may choose to insult by calling it
knotweed, goat's rue, Mexican devil, or stinking iris,
and uprooting it or stomping out its face,

merely ponder the possibility, dear friend,
as you traipse through the local woods and gardens,
it is you yourself who's in the wrong place.

A Boulder Has a Brain of Sorts

A boulder has a brain of sorts
with thoughts slower, but deeper than man can have,
but its firm unspeaking solidity

holds a bolstering force for us.
Loneliness and loss are always mixed up with glory,
and in its stolid lack of emotion

we find us free us to ponder in place,
unbudging, not hysterical, aggregated, of property.
I shall never dive into a fumerole.

Lament on a Deathbed

> "There was never great sadness, just a
> hint of sadness, before the tremendous
> wisdom of approaching death."
> —Etienne Leroux, *18/44*

A great part of the agony of dying
is surely that, plagued by remorse,
we sadly failed for want of trying
living up to Nature when its course
of innocence and unstained purity
openly received us while we lived,
heedless of its goodness, its surety,
and of its vernal holiness deprived.
Still, regret for all that we misplace,
born of late if heartfelt self-reproach
may yet constitute sufficient grace
and promise of redemption broach.
Nature renews everything that lives,
so by renewal its nature all forgives.

Dorothy Wrinch

Consider the faces we squire through life
with no alternative options, mere slaves
to every last windstorm of pain and strife
to be borne like a hump to our graves.

One can say yours was no Giotto mosaic,
let's face it, nor fit for a bold Cavalieri,
with a profile blunt as a stone and prosaic,
low-lit by eyes quite as empty as eerie.

I classify your beak an off-premise sign,
which I ignore to avoid having to cringe
with hair hysterically thraved and malign,
shaped like a butt with its lunatic fringe.

Your sole boast in life, we are damned sure,
is, unlike those forced to share in your space
as Vermonters can't say of New Hampshire,
something you yourself don't have to face.

Jews Fleeing Germany, 1943

Fear is ever a flight going south
in the vitals and makes escape in a body
like a bewildering grapevine,

as green and brown as diarrhea,
running fast as refugees through the route
of dark circuitous catacombs

recommended by other piraticals
to the intertwining Ore Mountains between
Germany and Czechoslovakia,

into Prague, by train to Genoa,
finally, to Paris, the down to rude Marseilles
to the Freeport of Lisbon

to board a ship to New York City,
fleeing Gestapo cellars or concentration camps,
fearing all the while a *south-up* map,

upside-down and reversed, in your groin
bringing you back by your terrifying nightmares
whereby all great fear goes north.

Shenandoah, Age Four, in Crisis

Shenandoah desperately weeps
over the sad reality of cartoon Wilbur being
unreal, very badly wanting to hug

(she gestures) the pig she keeps
alive with love, not that ideal she is seeing,
squeezing me (in proxy) with a tug.

Rosalie Pitou and the Cedar Tree

What a bold cedar tree trunk with its musculature,
told young brokenhearted Rose that freezing night

after breaking up with her boyfriend, left all alone
on a campus hill, surrounded by pitchy evergreens

ribbed exactly like a male's member, soft umber
brown in hue, but elongated, furrowed, rigid, tall,

was that symbols have a strategy for ruining life
by standing in the way of everything you'd avoid

to save yourself reflection, and, murdering hope,
carve deathly reflections in your soul bitten into

like script on seventeenth-century tombstones, very like
those on the hill there under rising cedars priapic

and perpendicular. She sat weeping, mute, staring
at the cedar tree trunk as empty as all emblems are,

praying that in *her* reality *she* could stand, show
her muscle, walk away, that *she* be green again.

Nothing is as astringent as a deodar to needle,
to pitch, but love is symbol, she saw, her man

what made it so, and there on the hill a scent
wafting from that cedar with bold musculature,

equally an image, a mark, a sign, one empty
enough to fill (which is just what symbols do),

blew hope into her heart and an image of a chest
she might still receive. So, she hugged the tree.

War in Afghanistan

A war begun in 2001,
every strategy unstrung,

45 billion bucks a year,
no U.S. plan ever clear

but to maintain chaos,
insure endless pathos,

at 2372 soldiers killed,
not a promise fulfilled,

31,000 civilians dead,
citizens going unfed,

the Taliban biding time
with acts of daily crime,

pious, waiting, clever,
our illogic to dissever;

the land itself so old,
craggy, cryptic, bold,

will in the end remain,
unforgiving its terrain,

and after all the shock?
Rubble, remnants, rock.

Mrs. Quark and Her Kids

Mrs. Quark with warm embraces
takes her kids Up, Down, Charm, Strange, Bottom,
and Top all to strut and swing

with a glockenspiel of wee faces
smiling inside shiny jackets of protons and neutrons
and vibrating a-quiver like string

go jigalooping wild along spaces
like any atomic family without a particle of difference
and, proving they matter, they sing.

Katharine Hepburn

"Sometimes I wonder if men and women really suit each other. Perhaps they should live next door and just visit now and then."

—K. H.

Katharine Hepburn could never play convincing mothers—
Violet Venable, Eleanor of Aquitaine, and Mary Tyrone,

to name but three, were dragons, Amanda Wingfield soft
as brie and Southern. (Neither could Kate do accents well.)

She relentlessly wore trousers, very like ironworkers do
and for interviews always kept one leg up, to brazenly sit

crotch-forward, that updangling limb, with white socks
and sandals—lesbian chic—an icon all the florid gays

cherished as a bold symbol of *fake* domineering moms
fey inverts have long deep-down made their girlfriends,

strong-willed and hoydenish, firedrakes all her poofters
adored who felt a thrill when Kate called them "Buster!"

and willingly forgave her when, sore as a boiled owl,
she screamed with sharp-clawed fits at awful reviews

or ordered them about and were word-perfect quoting,
"Norman, do you hear the loo-oons?" or "Dressing up

is a bo-aah!" or "The calla lilies are in blahoom again,
such a *straaange* flower, suitable to any occasion . . ." or

"Only when a woman decides not to have children,
can a woman live like a man. That's what I've done"

—which is why, frigid, determined against marriage,
she became in a twofold substitute Spencer Tracy's

mother, a man she pitied, a closet gay, an Irish drunk,
but never his wife (theirs was an utterly sexless union),

making up, *acting out*, the mother she could never be,
pretending to the public in face-flaking, voice-shaking

fabrications for *Screen Gems* and *Photoplay* and *Life*
that caretaking a moody alcoholic was true romance.

She knew absolutely nothing about men or sexuality
or God or children. What had a Woman of the Year

to do with nipples or nappies? Cosseting or coddling?
Kate adopted a boy, in a movie, only to polish her ego.

The deep truth is, the role of mother cannot be faked,
even in Hollywood terms, on screen, with makeup,

props, and lighting. But as to basilisks and wyverns,
gorgons, and hydras? That is something else entirely,

Lady Macbeth had at least once given suck! She knew
how tender it was to adore the baby that milked her

but swore, to prove a point, as it smiled in her face,
she'd pluck her wet nipple from its boneless gums

and dash its brains out. It was the one role Hepburn
(despite the accent) could have played to perfection.

Jane Birkin and Serge Gainsbourg

When the incandescent Jane Birkin
married homely Serge Gainsbourg,

him with a face like a dead quahog
and a proboscis like an ugly gherkin,

may I ask if her mind was working?
Was it a case of the hair of the dog

to so embrace a son of a synagogue
for some guilt in her darkly lurking?

I am aggrieved to see logic shirking,
that's all, in enigma's odd catalogue

to find a godly orchid in a dirty bog
and by marriage in mud interred in.

A Body Is But Cobbled Plans

I am 1.8 meters tall
weight of 95 kilograms
roughly 60% water

32 tough teeth, muscle,
of brains the milligrams
of the species otter,

7% blood all in all,
100 trillion cells, exams
of a microspotter,

much organ material
tissue, skin, epithelium,
fat, mineral matter,

of fluids a sprawl,
flesh, hormonal diagrams,
bone hard as mortar,

a bed of veins arterial,
wiring of nervous systems,
heart shape a quarter

of chambers, a ball,
beating of plasmaulic rams,
importer and exporter

of beauty and gall.
A body is but cobbled plans,
subject to disorder.

Effort Is Everything

When I heard the chewink in the hickory overhead,
—an eastern towhee, a finch—heartily trying to sing,

I smiled, for its song, limited to promising squeaks,
a short beginning, some squirts, gave nothing more

than a gawky attempt. It seemed to match the tree
neither in dereliction nor defeat but gormlessness,

a tree uncouth, odd, rigid, and scraggly. Its leaves
are always late—it equals the chewink's *yikyikyik*—

and drop early, although the finch's sleek colors,
black back, white breast, and light chestnut sides

improve upon the scaly shag of a tree that flakes.
The bark of any hickory is rags, its flowers small.

Poor little chewink builds its nests on the ground,
the tree is wind-pollinated and self-incompatible.

Difficult is hickory's globose or oval nut to open,
enclosed in a four-valved husk, divided in halves,

inaccessible, by comparison, as a chewink's song
lacking any melody and its frenzy failure to find it,

thick shelled both, brown in stain, a grain to turn
the blade of an axe, each full of something wrong

No, for song the bird is no musical song sparrow
or thrush. And yet both aim at crude straightness,

and for the bird its squeak or the tree its lateness
of leaf, a forlorn ragged look or inability to sing,

endeavoring to strive, to vie, aim, is never narrow.
The finding is in the seeking. Effort is everything.

The Beauty of America Is Its Space

American tourists pay millions, who love its congestion,
to take in Old World charm, by long centuries congealed,
its narrow streets, tall ramparts, a cramping compression,
towns all hedged-in, dim crooked lanes, piecemeal fields,
listing old guildhalls, shuttered lodgings, ancient bridges
of stone, clock towers high, rude stairways to cathedrals
at the far end of villages, compact with edges and ridges,
countries with borders reinforced by political upheavals.

Every locale in each region is bound as if surrounded by belts.
Wherever you go is around the corner from everywhere else.

Whereas in America, a New World, the order is reversed.
Open the door! Gaze westward! You can breathe space!
Wood, enchanted forests, in blessed bounty are dispersed.
Far prairies lead to summits, and, meeting, there embrace!
Nothing calls you round the corner, even the cities stroll,
mountains, farms, gold plains, unbroken miles of grass,
rivers, trails, peaks, endless vistas unfold, unfurl, unroll,
for freedom is an open space where you can freely pass.

No locale in these regions is bound as if surrounded by belts.
Wherever you go in true freedom is open to everywhere else.

Only When Kafka Was Ready to Die

Only when Kafka was ready to die
was the man willing to marry,

that he might avoid in future, or try,
with each misfortune to tarry,

and, so, with certainty say goodbye,
to two heavy burdens to carry.

John Singer Sargent

For Madame Gautreau
Sargent used raisin and claret-soaked plum
for that daring gown,

for *The Misses Vickers*
a fully rich palette of winter fruit compote
to get faces of down,

such worshipful beauty
incandescent enough to be embraced from
adorable feet to crown,

with colors on canvases
so pulpily painted to seem truly edible and
berry-bright as a clown.

Father Pedophile

Sadomasochistic isolationism,
disambiguated hypoexcusivism,
parthenogenetic antediluvianism
grew out of Roman Catholicism.

Ultrahedonistic eunuchoidism,
super paratistic isolationism,
chauvinistic authoritarianism
gave birth to homoeroticism.

Servomechanistic momism,
paternalistic neo-skepticism,
neorecidivistic parochialism,
encouraged ultra-narcissism.

Epicurean non-chrismaticism,
extremist sexual adventurism,
dysphemtistic eunuchoidism
led to chronic obstructionism.

A Character Is a Part

The thing is, any one of us could go around
in the Queen's body. She is she to inhabit it

as a figurehead, a name none couldn't have,
so, if Elizabeth II does go boasting about it,

she must also be told to admit that her name
is a role with a mask for the lady inside her.

Can anyone take credit for a role she takes
upon herself to fulfill what everyone wants

her to be to be able to recognize to salute?
A character is a *part*. The greater the role,

the less that person is who so assumes it.
If one takes away a mask to leave a face,

only then do we expect nothing majestic
a real person, with no necessity for grace.

Nelson Eddy, Kevin Costner, and Robert Taylor

> "Others act, but only thou dost speak."
> —(reverse paraphrase) Ben Jonson
> on actor Edward ("Ned") Alleyn

None of these fellows could act,
so instead they talked, unmysteriously,
as if, say, being in an elevator,

asking whether their smoking
bothered you or stating it was raining,
wooden voiced, no translator

necessary, no emotion, inflation,
nothing nuanced nor dramatic nor bold,
like suggestions from a waiter,

nothing at all to do with acting
style, and, as far as entertainment goes,
their banal chat a total deflator.

Depend Upon a Zebra

Children's book illustrators take refuge
in the alphabet—the go-to text for lazy minds—
and to prove it all use zebras for the Z,

stripes, insane face, the caboose drawing
that even toddlers expect, singing out its name!
I have seen all the zebras I can bear,

talking trains, monkeys making mayhem,
fat airplanes with crazy risible eyes looping over
grinning suns, moons, bulb-headed folk

doing jobs, milkmen, bakers, cobblers
in frenzied make-believe cities with all the streets
jammed with fire trucks, carts, and bikes,

landscapes pullulatingly alive. No farm
—or farmer—was ever that clean or cunningly cute,
no cop as joyful or obliging or so thin.

Q is always a quail, W is always a whale,
Y is forever a yak, and X is configured a xylophone
and, of course, sing song is always for sale.

Vegetables have dear faces, but in real life
who will ever be found to be as kind as Mr. Carrot
or any anthropomorphized banana or beet?

Toby the Tadpole, Harry the Horse, Gerty
and loping Georgy Giraffe are selling convention
more than anything else. Bold imagination

looks in vain to these hustling artistes,
ready with their crayons, to portray anything we know
for what they assume we want to be handed.

The irony is that everything is predictable.
in the goony way fables organize logic and morality.
Bank only on flash. Depend upon a Zebra.

Jody Arias

If a bond, a union, is held as sacred,
then a jealous lover's act is not immoral when,
finding herself rejected out of hand,

she kills the person she once loved,
a true idealism for perfection in a relationship
as a lost, scrupulous, decent stand,

honoring even if by default a vow,
illegal although any murder is, a fealty upheld,
a bond, if not the outcome planned.

Reality

You can only see a rainbow
if your back is to the sun.

To discover magic colors,
you must brightness shun.

Loss is never uninvolved
in something you have won.

A Barking Mother Terrifies Her Young

A barking mother terrifies her young,
breeding both panic and terror borne
by the sharpness of a lashing tongue
and angry unforgiving eyes of scorn.
Any mad bellowing leveled at a child
guarantees for sure a legacy of pain,
for fright so echoes in a mind defiled
that, even should it happen not again,
it yet portends with promising alarm,
in a child now grown alert with dread.
No honeyed words undo such harm.
Screams hollow out a victim's head
Do they obey, quote her out of fear?
How they act shows how they scare.

Fame Sucking

Celebrity ultimately proves empty as a cenotaph.
Queen Victoria wanted George Eliot's autograph,

and, concerning the relative arbitrariness of glare,
Jacqueline Kennedy the same of Claudette Colbert.

Older Parents

Abraham, the Bible says,
was eighty-six years old,

for as go passing days
small miracles unfold,

when first son Ishmael
was born by slave Hagar

who held, or so Jews tell,
to their hearts a dagger,

preferring Isaac instead,
born by Sarah at ninety,

that their nation be led
by this son more likely.

Old Abe then dismissed
both first son and slave,

letting caprice persist
and fatherly love waive.

Drifted they in desert
food locust and scarab,

clothed in goat hair shirt
as wore the nomad Arab.

As far as awful parents
go, this one as a sample

for provable aberrance,
let old age be example.

Shipbuilder Oak

For a framing wood,
full sturdy, bespoke,

choose a pasture oak
alone, where it stood,

that had no protection
from all blowing wind,

(unwarped, unskinned)
from whatso direction

where the dur sapwood
is all cleanly diffused,

with no side recused
it grows as it should

round its wood heart,
a sapwood is tougher

and faraway rougher—
its fibers won't part—

than any heart wood
and all timber made

from this oak is good
to keep a storm stayed.

The trunk is its own,
its roots to its height

created where grown
alone in God's sight.

Judas

Only "one of the Twelve:"
no further identification of him
served than who was who.

Restraint of description
was sufficient for vice, leaving
him but one of the few,

on whom fewer words
being spent heightened the evil
where dark evil grew.

No curses or loud prompts
no vocables to accrue. Enough
to say, only, you were you.

The Colors of Paul Bowles

A lavender man feeding off black thoughts
under the tangerine Tangier sun loved North Africa,
where snobbery allowed any person white

to speak blue Berber in scarlet flesh pots,
where in yellow decadence, every lout a trafficker,
gays cruised brown Arab boys all night.

Owlage

Their face is an ear, round as the moon.
the cochlea an open window to hearing

any whisper or twitch in an ebon forest
which gives every barn owl swift wing

to swing feather-soft through any night
despite its darkest modes, velvet quiet,

faint of noise, wings downy rabbit fur,
velvet, muted, breaking up turbulence

in flight, to detect by its auditory sense
burrowing voles three feet under snow

to snatch them up with its killer talons
and with nib-beaks sharp as ice-cutters

shred them ricey. As to owlish eyesight,
their bold eyes are locked, and so to see

they must swerve their head, swiveling
the plate-shaped conk, concave noddle,

all at once, eyes, mouth, acute earholes,
and barbaric beak, a snatching machine!

Soft and hard, both velvety and vicious,
Who are you, owl? I mean, *how* are you?

Pot Roast

Flabby in its dirty burrow,
a woodchuck is the true hibernator,
hunking in his sleepy deep

with its fat bulbous blanket
worn like the grizzled brown pelage
that hugs the rodent in fur

as a defense against the cold
triggering the hibernating instinct
under the cold down ground

where nothing will wake it,
breathing once every ten minutes
but very vitally alive there—

unaware, as a bottom round,
slow-cooked, with some heady herbs
my dinner ambitions are clear—

in a dark quiet solemn grave
its body temperature at 40 degrees
a good chuck is warm as toast.

Is he dreaming of food as I am
of him, filled with fresh grass, plants,
of a splendiferous brown roast?

Robert Frost Throwing Pennies

At times, poet Robert Frost declared
that from a crazy antic impulse of his

as a sort of revolt against the poverty
in which he and his wife Elinor lived,

and delighting in thoughts of the joy
small boys'd have picking them up,

or so he claimed, he'd hurl pennies,
dimes, and nickels by the handful

into schoolyards and into the streets
of Lawrence, Mass. In point of fact,

it was a *needy* act, and desperate,
by which he really sought to gain

as much love as he could purchase
to do away with all his inner pain.

Departure Always Leaves a Hollow Freedom

Departure always leaves a hollow freedom,
for in the heart the need to *be*, by the lights
of the way hard life comes to us at random,
seeks a sense, as to stability, in what unites
rather than the waywardness that separation,
by so forcing us to be alone in all we face,
reveals as well how, at its heart, termination
which both gives and takes a kind of grace,
leaves us, while being free, also feeling lost.
Who says goodbye, the openness of liberty
attends with new emptiness that has a cost
by affirming one feels alone quite bitterly.
In any state of emptiness what must follow
is that vacancy's another word for hollow.

Miss Hudnut's Trees

"The saddest thing in life is that the
best thing in it should be courage."
—Robert Frost

Edna Hudnut, listening to the radio
where the voice of Raymond G. Swing
brought terrible news of World War II

through the brooding console—
its dark bulkiness in a corner of the room,
the grim aspect of nightly bleak reports—

heard of GIs being slaughtered,
one a special youth she knew from Truro,
for whom she planted a sapling

—they might have become close,
but she timidly lost her nerve at a dance
when he asked to walk her home,

a possibility, until she saw him
speaking to another girl, when painfully
her renewed pluck came too late—

and, after another year of reports
bringing far more deaths and Swing's voice
from Britain, she planted more trees,

but try as Edna might after hard work,
in trying to establish a wider stand of apples,
Cole's Quinces, Sweet Boughs,

and Porter, scions, many old varieties,
grafting them as a neighbor had taught her,
nothing whatsoever came of it all,

even though leaving by the bent stile
he had waved his hat and cried, *"Courage,"*
before loping over the blue hill,

for she had planted too late in the Fall
and by re-digging to re-plant, shovel-slavery
of a kind bombed-out war refugees

in bombed-out Europe only too well knew,
she made it only worse. She wept in a corner,
facing away from the brutal console,

where seeing the old failures of her trees
outside seemed to say *trying*, alone, was sadly
what courage meant, soulless repetition.

Reverend Stone Shallcross

The Reverend gave deathly dull sermons.
Was he a Christian? He would never make pastoral visits
to any and all non-members or any of those

who, despairing every single Sunday,
tense in a pew as they listened to the ranting overkill,
could not help but leave his church.

It was OPC but closer to Baptist in what
the pastor condemned, things like Christmas and Easter,
feast days that he found far too Catholic.

At the Presbyterian church, on their knees,
congregants all through the winter prayed for the soul
after around Hallowe'en he was rusticated

to Ohio after confessing an impropriety,
in the pulpit, bedraggled, tearful, hands pointed overhead
like a dunce cap. Nobody knew his fault.

Was it embezzlement? Had he caught ahold
of one of the Bible Study women? How had he crossed the line?
One day he returned to the fold, sheepishly

to begin anew. He now wore a short beard.
and lifts. He made up in volume what he lacked in intelligence,
as he preached the Gospels with fire and flame.

He still fancied himself a strict Puritan,
the real kind, like earnest John Bunyan and his allegory
of wooden souls plodding the earth—

he kept multiple copies of *Pilgrim's Progress*
in his office where he plugged away the week through
on his dry-as-dust sermons, finicking finely

with his faith, while seven kids bleating in his
messy house whooped at play. Fay Shallcross made muffins
for the Sunday after-service coffees

held in the church lobby, a sad, sleepy wife,
always pregnant, whose brain seemed badly to be missing.
Mrs. Tablett, angry, once upbraided him

after an hour of his preaching as not being
truly OPC! The congregation with wide eye-watering yawns
gawped out the windows as, barking away,

Pastor Shallcross proof-texted his Bible,
yammering on about Habakkuk, Nahum, Hosea, Malachi,
"He could never slay the bull," said Roy Bone

to Ferty Ricepaw years after he and the Mrs.
not only left the church but even walked away from the faith,
missing only the fresh blueberry muffins,

which after leaving church he often took home,
a place that the Pastor never once bothered again to visit,
they felt, wounded, in a most un-Christian way.

Porcupines in the Trees

Porcupines have a positive need of trees
who have a never-ending craving for salt
and to highest limb a quill-pig can vault
like any agile climber with relative ease

chewing out bark for its favorite flavors
tight gripping the salty bark like a vice
licking alkali, sodium, brine, zest, spice
from pines, willows, hemlocks it savors

with a rough bark less tasty than smooth
finding in woodsalt's sharp sweet sweat
what like a response to a tart vinaigrette
wakens the spines to which it gives tooth

biting off bark that on its tongue tickles
sending dopamine musk to a crazy brain
which infuses much of the exquisite pain
into the barbs of its razor-sharp prickles.

Twin Needles

Pine needles come in bundles of two,
suggesting to me in a binding way
of the way of love with me and you,
as in all seasons they primly stay,

but both are brittle and easily break
when rain beats down or cold sets in
to warn me too that a strength within
needs to adhere for the others' sake.

Sugaring Time

When a sugar bush of forest maples
sends a scent of sap in rainy March

in the roaring heft of northwest wind
and 40-odd degrees of steady cold

is maintained in an atmosphere bold
with tree buds tight seem also skinned

as your own fingers as stiff as starch—
behold, New England sugaring staples.

The Delight in Being Wrong

A child is scrupulous to the lyrics of song.
When substituting the wrong word in a nursery rhyme,
you can see their eyes brimming with joy,

as they fall back to cackle "You're *wrong!*"
Throw in a false lyric or silly name—I do it every time
as if by wry intention, an underhanded ploy—

you will never once find them playing along
(or is gulling you exactly the role they have in mind?).
Girls find you more idiotic if you are a boy

which is the case in our household throng,
with Shiloh and Shenny who tingle out like a chime
when any error is heard and are never coy

to set you straight with a ping and a pong!
"Noooo, you made a MISTAKE!" they cry on a dime,
delighted to humble you, but mostly annoy,

for they wait with planned glee all day long
to wag a finger at you like some professional mime,
and with "You're *wrooooong*, Daddy!" convoy

with a scream as sharp as any harpoon prong.
"You made a lie!" Shall I be honest? Mine's the crime.
Their wild, wild delight is fully mine to enjoy.

Gannet Girl

> The Yoruba say, "*Eniyan bi aparo ni omo araye n' fe*," meaning the world loves a person who is like a partridge. The partridge is a poor bird that, enfeebled by its creation, has little ability to hunt, gather, protect, or feed itself.

"I want to live where there are no niggers,"
declared the racist professor at Yale, Deuteronomy Talbot
when she saw my Mass. license plates—

she was fed up with the vicious crime
that she saw pullulating not only in downtown New Haven
but in all the now unsafe American streets—

"move to Norway or Bhutan or Siberia
to live a safe life, removed from thievery, crazy behavior,
the endless sordid news reports of violent rape

and live where all those northern gannets
in their avian wisdom choose to live, where *they* choose
to thrive, clean, white, cold, fresh, happy,

perhaps the United Kingdom, which boasts
about two thirds of the world's population of joyful gannets
and their important nesting grounds,

or Scotland, including the Shetland Isles,
Canada, Ireland, Faroe Islands, Iceland, the Bay of Biscay,
the Channel Islands, or that single colony—

I checked—in Germany called Heligoland.
There is not a single successful black nation on the planet!
But how could there be, they idly loaf,

sitting on their fat asses, waiting for free handouts,
sucking dope pipes, loudly jiggling coins in their pockets
in ferret-filthy doorways. *What bird on earth*

would stand for this? They are too dignified!
I want to move out from this crooked and benighted city,
replete with drugs, broken fences, sewers

backed up, Burger Kings filled with coons
stacked up on each other in booths howling for hamburgers,
howling police sirens, gangs roaming the streets,

hip-hop music, the vile orts and sorts of aliens,
pork-pie-hatted Hottentots without a brain, inferior trash,
and not a gannet in sight! *I want them near me*,

beautiful white birds in a clean and sane world
who use their webbed feet to warm their eggs, to breathe
the air of islands and coasts into my own soul."

White Cargo

> "This is a generation of wingless chickens."
> —Flannery O'Connor

What in behavior is the proper way to hew?
It is harder by far to love than to command.
when the matter of pleasing comes to hand.
Duty does as commandments make us do,
we find, and so discover with great relief
to learn commandments can replace love,
to recognize, with emotion to dispose of,
that fought faith can cede to plain belief.

What a comfort to be told the way to act,
relieved of any heavy burden to be free,
that one may emerge from choice intact
without weakness of defense unbacked.
Let precepts, edicts, rules, and orders be.
Best my response be your responsibility.

Norma Jean Baker

It was the *inner* child, her purity, paradoxically,
that made Marilyn Monroe the sexual icon that she became,
not the opposite, distinguishing her in every way

from other bottle blondes such as Jayne Mansfield
and Mamie Van Doren, an image that was based on a reality
of a deprived girl in constant need of a father figure,

according to the damaged girl's real-life needs,
a deep-seated entail, a plea, for a daddy as evidenced by
the older men she sought and in cases married.

The waif beneath the movie star, a foundling outcast,
the underprivileged, the strapped, the disadvantaged stray
endearing mudlark—*her*, we wanted badly to hold.

Caruso Begrudged the City of Naples

Caruso begrudged the city of Naples,
long a center for grand opera staples,

although he was born there in 1873,
of a very large family poor but free.

In 1894 he was mocked off the stage
by an audience dismissive with rage

on his first appearance at the age twenty-one,
just when his early career had begun,

a hostile reception because an affront
was taken by some critics grown blunt

for his having first appeared in Milan,
and, so, he was duly met with a yawn

and panned as a singer, dim, uncouth,
no small rebuff for a sensitive youth,

and ever thereafter the tenor omitted
visiting there, quite firmly committed

was he that indeed he did never return,
with two exceptions, a double concern,

to visit his mother on one chosen day
and to eat some *vermicelli alle vongole*.

Famous in town, Caruso was sought,
but the wounded singer never forgot

just how he was met when but a lad
by prig, by snob, by lout, and by cad,

and so by vow he sang there no more
although fans would beg and implore.

He sang to all. But of Naples as venue?
Sorry, that item was not on the menu.

No One Sins for No Cause at All

> "A friendship unfriendly, unanalyzable
> attraction for the mind..."
> —St. Augustine

No one sins for no cause at all.
Wickedness becomes a joy in itself.
The appeal to the self is to appall,
To feel the sense in the self to fall.
It hints by a measure at being tall.
Rebellion has an aspect of health.

The malice of any act that is base
Is sought by choice an end in itself.
To commit sin is to court disgrace
In the joy of wearing another face,
By putting two selves into one race,
To offer a mind double the wealth.

There is a terrible beauty in sin,
Offering pride a loftiness of spirit,
And by some perverse revel within
A delight to be outside looking in,
Fleeing salvation, damnation's twin,
To be redeemed by way of demerit.

We savor a vanity in being pursued,
Putting the soul beyond God's reach,
Like that one sheep lost, so to elude
The loving shepherd to be subdued,
To feel within us with full certitude
A perverse glory in making a breach.

Storms Make Me Feel Wonderful

Storms make me feel wonderful.
Revelations sing in me under an angry sky
bloating iron-coal-gray with rain,

relieving me of any present pain
and providing a dangerous possibility to try
shrugging off everything effortful,

for when fire-bolts crack white gold
dark clouds thunder over an upwelling ocean
I come alive with blood turned green

and, lo, am relieved of all my spleen
finding below as above the turbulent motion
that lights up my vision seven-fold.

Patriotism

"The moment there is a misunderstanding
about a boundary line or a hamper of fish or
some other squalid matter, see Patriotism
rise, & hear him split the universe with a
war-whoop."
—Mark Twain

Word it as softly as you please,
the barbaric spirit of patriotism

in any full bellow for any ism
especially in its mode to seize

is the spirit of the dog and wolf,
its teeth open ferociously to bite,

always assuming a higher height,
to attack, devour, quickly engulf.

There is in pig-headed blindness
an insistent, self-righteous need

to define virtue in terms of greed
with nothing at all of refinedness

or any grace. It thumps the table
with boasts and tinny gasconade

that of nations one alone is able
—ordained—to lead the parade,

better than all, richer, and brave,
worthiest and, as proof, its might

is the reason it is worthy to fight,
conquer, prevail, others enslave

Nationalism is the cause of war,
its voice a cruel croak of fustian.

No patriot can be a true Christian,
no God exists he claims to speak for.

1763

Molasses was made into West Indian rum,
most of it was shipped off to distant Africa

to be traded and bartered for field negroes,
who were shipped in turn to the Caribbean

to be sold to cut sugarcane and grow beets
in order to make molasses for Indian rum.

No One Can Ride Like the Blackfeet

No one can ride like the Blackfeet,
who merge in a round communion

as they lean looped on their horses,
galloping into the fierce blue wind

to circle the wilds of Saskatchewan
with open mouths as round as wide,

around their heads sporting a band,
hoop with a bead, ring with a ball,

disk of feathers, like a magic globe,
arms round the horse, circlet coiled,

a loud thunderation of oval gallops
astride a horse going round around

as open and free as the rolling dawn
to circle the wilds of Saskatchewan.

Igbok Karatoprak Was a Noted Chiropractor

Igbok Karatoprak was a noted chiropractor
who functioned by his hand, but a big factor

in his practice when ministering to an actor
was a lust he felt whene'er he smacked her,

releasing in passion hot sprays of aerobacter,
which so confused and began to distract her

that each consult re-proved him a detractor
then a perverted, down-and-out malefactor,

but, after police came to question the reactor,
jailed Karatoprak was no longer a transactor.

As I Go Walking in Paris, I Hear the Bells

As I go walking in Paris, I hear the bells,
echo as a savor of wine within me swells,

their peals evoking such sweetness in air
that I feel I can actually taste what I hear.

Pouilly-Fuissé, Petrus, une Clape Cornas
Chateau La Mission Haut Brion, Fanasse

Bourgueil, Verget Batard Montrachet
Une Chateau Lagrezette Le Pigeonnier

Château Haut-Brion Pessac-Léognan
Domaine Leroy Corton Charlemagne

Château Cheval Blanc Saint Émilion
Une Moet et Chandon Dom Perignon

Domaine Romanée Conti Echezaux
Vosne-Romanee, Aligote, Margaux

Une Chateau Suduiraut, Pétrus Pomerol,
Zind Humbrecht Riesling Clos Windsbuhl

As I go walking in Paris I hear the bells,
and inherit the magic each of them tells

with my sight and touch also made clear
that I feel I can actually taste what I hear.

Over a Lifetime I Have Eaten Ten Cows

I have wolfed down brisket, burgers ground,
meatloaf, bangers, rib-eye steaks without omission,
beef clod, ribs, chuck, filet, top of the round,

brains, kidneys, tongue, including their milk,
in short, *eaten ten cows in full* by my own admission,
and twice an eyeball that went down like silk.

If we should rendezvous in heaven to stare,
will a renewal of the cows and me prove a recognition
of ten happy partners or a lowing despair?

No Photograph Can Ever Capture Duration

No photograph can ever capture duration.
It sees only the glum, what's in front of it.

It can never capture a full truth of the sea,
fat mountains, far too wide in perspective,

too cold and long for the mimicking eye
that blinks like a coward at Nature in full

and is mimicked like any tool that wobbles,
its horizon restricted like a wet human eye

Forget span, length, extent, spell, stretch,
perpetuation, anything like continuance

from its fast action fribbles, clicks, clacks,
and clucks. Vastness of time *alone* reveals

the infinite vastness that poor photography
claims to be showing to memory in a snap,

shot by what's mocked by true persistence,
which alone is disclosed by a laughing God.

Chantal Destroismaisons

To know her was to know
animals eat with a sense of stealing.
To rob is nature's first exhortation,
if it isn't kill or be killed,

and purloining, as she defined it,
—skittering away, your soul scooped out—
was a form of embroidery.
May I purl your loins, my friend?

Cheeriness gave her thefts
the breezy air of free delivery
until you found yourself charged
double. No, she was a chipmunk,

skittering off, you unaware,
with cheeps of delight, a nut
in the rictus of a stoplit-red mouth,
extorted as if it were her very own,

for colposcoping anyone
she saw, leaving no recovery time,
gave her sense of stealing
merely but a meal nature offered.

The animal joy of stealing
imparts the kind of success
that snatching mimes the embroidery
of delighted complication.

The Perennial Is Not the Eternal

Nothing has a neighbor nearer than God.
One can feel it in the forest with the trees
and in the woodlands where they're shod,
rising to the holy sun by strange degrees.
I look upon them with reverence and awe
but do not confuse creation with Creator,
for no truly steadfast believer ever saw
the great to then mistake it for the greater.
A visionary experiences nature as a gift,
lavish moments of far deeper infinitude
of majesty through which he seeks to sift
but never limit the Designer's amplitude.
The world, lit by the sun's vast territory,
lasts but seconds to God's eternal glory.

Creation Is But a Part of the Majesty of God

Creation is but a part of the majesty of God.
The world we know that the pantheist exalts
is but a fraction of it, his celebrations flawed
by a restricted vision narrowed by defaults.
Nature is but an *instant* of God's strength,
Indeed, the universe but a second's power
regarding his height and width and length,
that only folly would measure by the hour.
The absolute vanity of determining divine
what we praise in forests, mountains, seas
is to limit God's greater glory and so assign
deity to a leaf, a stone, any passing breeze.
Never limit praise of God to mere elation.
God's grandeur exceeds his own creation.

Wicked Boy

The boy Wordsworth was never ill
—is never being ill a fury to survive?—
and even as an old man walked
upwards of thirty miles a day
over hardly a yard of level ground.

He was naughty, wild, vital, alive
with animal spirits, all diagnosed
as wickedness by his maternal grandparents
the Cooksons from Penrith, drapers,
an unamiable couple and severe

who belittled and whipped him
when he lived with them to the age of nine,
after his own father passed away,
in a what he felt to be a prison house,
a purgatory, a hell on earth.

The couple kept him from knowing
songs and legends, separated him from,
Dorothy, his sister whom he loved and missed,
and he was never at ease with the poor,
or social inferiors, other folk

but chose instead to wander and walk,
for feeling ill would have kept him home,
and he walked to heal his inner wounds.
Nature became protective armor for him
His poetry was all composed on his feet.

Wandering lonely, he turned to nature
from mankind, to escape the human,
the urban, the authoritarian, fleeing
more from something that he dreaded
than pursuing the thing he loved,

all a quick escape route from Penrith
and the bad-tempered draper and his wife
to the mountains and lakes that
serving as a consolatory function
kept him sane, naughty, wild, vital

alive—healthy—an acute, acute, acute,
for being able to go wandering was to survive.
That vigor was but a lad being astute
that vivaciousness beneath a fury,
to keep himself, a naughty wicked boy, alive.

Shiloh and Shenandoah at Age Five

In the same way that birdsong is landscape,
five-year-old girls create both vista and sweep

of a lovely land that will never be seen again:
soft kisses, pure delight in waking from sleep,

taking the stairs on padded feet, leaping about
sand dunes, squealing at waves of the tidal sea,

twins so happily reinforced within and without
that they understand each other as me and me

—true-blue Cape Codders, both Shen and Shi
have seen an actual whale, stranded on shore—

drawing castles, singing songs as they swing,
biting Charleston Chews, and asking for more,

sticky hands, a need to whirl, riddles to invent
("Is your refrigerator running?"), facial socks,

hair the scent of lilacs, princesses of any sort,
skipping through a meadow, pocketing rocks,

a fascination to correct you, crying *"Nooo!"*
giggling at anything, chocolate on their nose,

jumping into the possibility of any photograph
with a Hollywood model's hearty need to pose,

dancing with great fistfuls of animal crackers,
squirming wherever they sit, a love of ditties,

o'er-leaping like clowns on sofas and pillows,
tweaking your nose, mock-yowling like kitties,

mispronouncing words ("Where's Yew Nork,"
"Mommy sampled"—not stapled—"the paper,"

arranging elaborate structures with curtains
with the expertise of the best Parisian draper,

taking your temperature, stating, "40-784!"
loud as foghorns at the pitch of their delight,

drawing faces, figures, in the Basquiat mode,
their pigtails bobbing while their flying a kite

squealing in a bath like two waterborne sprites
dancing up and down when eating Mason Dots,

their dramatic hugs warmer than Mount Etna's fire,
settling hot arguments by logically drawing lots.

To see again their faces every morning is to feel
that waking each day truly carries new meaning,

as if Spring explodes anew in each bud and bloom
to reveal hills and valleys suddenly re-greening,

a world redeemed as so was the case with Noah,
their breath sweeter than the winds of Samoa,

their mellow eyes, their hair soft as a feather boa.
So go some thoughts on Shiloh and Shenandoah.

Flammable Cladding

What of the belief in the futility of raising children
in an unimprovable world? What sanctuary have they to survive?
What cladding to protect them from fire?

Ezra Pound, who thought motherhood damaged women,
rendering them unfit for anything else, tended to dislike children.
Less fit creatures are meant to be parents, not artists,

he felt. After his mistress Olga Rudge gave birth
to a daughter, she and Pound handed her over to a peasant woman
in the maternity ward who raised Mary on her own.

In Paris, Pound and his wife Dorothy Shakespear
even refused to allow children in their studio. George Eliot, who
believed in duty but not in God or immortality,

saw her writing as an actual form of parturition,
an aspect of godhood, but upon being delivered of one of her books
felt deserted, but a poor husk, dried out and used up.

Was this childless woman determined to avoid
being devoured by a voracious needy infant, its demanding yowls,
preferring the voice instead of her own creativity?

Or was foremost in her mind the overarching fear
that bringing new life to this cold world, a blasphemy? Is fearing
children closer to love than hating them, the terror

of feeling inadequate to shelter, screen, secure, love,
and protect them? Motherhood *does* damage a woman in all she
feels of obligation, surely. But then artists who seek

a lordly parenthood by creation, Ezra, Olga, and Dot,
must have sensed that miming nature by excluding any children
is mocking art and, when compared to fecund nature,

nothing but sheer futility, unimprovably a dead end,
with no sanctuary to survive, a world damaged and ignominiously
brought to a flaming halt by the seduction of sterility.

I despair in recalling that V.S. Naipaul once declared
that he thought the ugliest thing on earth was a pregnant woman,
speaking of unimprovable worlds, unimprovable churls.

Sharp Leaves

A holly tree's more yellow in June than green
shedding its dead and dying leaves
that come swirling down in a paradoxical scene
as if from a traitorous act it grieves.

Why at the height of summer colors transpose
so is a mystery, expect that yellow
has ever been to green among its fiercest foes
and, sadly, characteristic of a fellow.

Stalin Loved to Munch on Roasted Bear

Stalin loved to munch on roasted bear.
He always presided at the left of the head of the table
to keep a weather eye on any foes,

being suspicious of poisons, as well,
extending to the great gouts of the black meat he pawed,
while yamphing cuts already tasted

by any number of other unctuous eaters
like scary overweening Beria or chubby Malenkov.
"Don't—never—look into his eyes"

was a long-held rule they all followed
which set off his paranoia, born of childhood beatings
by his intemperate father. Drinking

is Russian; he brought his own wine,
bottles from the Caucasus and gulped it, sitting high
there on the left, his weather eye keen,

after chops, on a gloppy dish he invented
called Aragvi, mutton with aubergines, tomatoes, potatoes.
Later, his bad teeth forced him to mump

the softest pieces of lamb and the ripest fruits
which he often grabbed by hands smelling of gamy bear,
predatory, the way he yanked the heads

of rivals who, looking at him far too long,
spilling their plates of soup filled with crumbled bread,
and twisted them, laughing at his power

before sending them off to the Lubianka
to be shot. The length his reach extended! Where he sat
ripping into his black cuts of roasted bear

with his Kamchatka molars was exactly where
no one else should have been near who yearned to keep alive
beyond the reach of his wet predator paws.

Jesus in Egypt

The gift of gold one of the Magi presented
to the Holy family was surely used to travel to Egypt
when threated by rabid Herod, ready to slay

every boy under the age of two lest the crown
fall to a usurper ready one day to seize his Judean throne
and preen like a cock in his own royal array,

for how else afford a distant journey, although
hoping to return when that madman died, as soon he did,
so, after an announcing angel opened the way

they spent three long years in the faraway sands,
until after a dream Joseph led them all back to Palestine,
infant Jesus, mankind's Redeemer and émigré.

Henry Thoreau Doesn't Become a Catholic

Isaac Hecker, a baker at Brook Farm and vision-haunted,
after becoming a resident of Concord, needed to find digs

and so took a room in Cynthia Thoreau's boarding house,
where he continued to undertake a long spiritual journey

and, as days passed, pursued a friendship, or call it that,
with the "stiffish" Henry who habitually walked by him

in the parlor, not out of rudeness, but being preoccupied
elsewhere, as he often was, out on the water, in forests.

"It's only by forgetting *yourself* you draw near to God,"
Henry said to Ike, wandering back home late one night

finding him sitting (crusading?) on the dark front porch,
idling in a swing chair. "It is not"—why dodge further?—

"when I am going to meet him," he said, regarding God,
"but when I am just turning away and leaving him alone

that I discover what God is. I say God," added Henry,
"I am not sure that that's the name." Isaac just sat there

as Henry called back, "You will know what I mean,"
and he did just that, turning away to leave both alone,

God to his own good purposes and Isaac to his faith,
who joined the Catholic Church, going even so far

as to found the Paulist Society and whenever asked
about his friend always said, "A 'consecrated crank.'"

Drowned in Nova Scotia

The Bay of Fundy
where the incoming sea sucks loud
with the sound of kissing,

which many describe
alternately in a more hideous way
as a serpent hissing

still fiercely remains
with its incoming tides the occasion
of one soul missing.

Suicide Notes Are Almost Always Inconsequential

Suicide notes are almost always inconsequential.
No thoughts at the time can fix on the indignity

or the newness of the uncanny horror taking place
to vet the scribbles for logic, intention, or subject,

no matter the means chosen to bring about death.
The mind is far too scrambled to find any reason,

any one reason—this is all about *accumulation*—
to be making such a momentous decision. Focus

of prose, to be able in a zero to express thoughts
or deep feelings one felt unable to express in life,

compositional details, are not what I'm addressing
here, like the need to dissipate guilt in oneself

or the mad urge to increase pain of all survivors
or to give pat instructions for disposal of remains

or grimly to confess to an act of murder or rape.
"My hamster will need celery" is what is noted

usually as the incidental, inessential irrelevancy
swiftly penned. "Go to the old box in the cabinet

to find a 1972 Lincoln penny for Susan Poker,
who wanted it" or—irrelevant, immaterial, minor,

trivial, silly, piddling, insubstantial paltry, trifling,
nugatory, lightweight—"Hug a balloon for me"

or "Who will win the World Series, the Red Sox?"
or "The pot roast on the stove is for my husband,

Heshie with irritable bowel syndrome and won't eat"
or "Kill every Republican!" It is far too abhorrent

to center one's attention on what witty W. C. Fields
referred to as "The Man in the Bright Nightgown,"

never directly or with eloquence or graceful words.
Easier to bow out as a side-issue, tossing off a quip.

A suicide note is almost always a *non-sequitur*,
like *not* saying goodbye, before you shut door.

Malfeasance

If as Rabbi Isaac Luria declared in 1572
that God in order to make room for the world
yielded space filled by his own presence,

how can a divine creation be so off true
as over ages, brimming and replete, it swirled
when permeated by such Godly essence,

or is it the case that if God withdrew
to leave a human stew so knotted and knurled
blame befall him for *his* malfeasance?

Shakespeare's Forests
a sonnet

Magical is a forest in Shakespeare's view,
unknowable of recess and of haunting cave,
its dark wildness real, distinct, pied of hue,
where old branches linked in crossing trave
camouflage acts of shifting transformation,
as ghosts rise to haunt each running stream
alive with feints, disguise, tricks, striation,
and, making mystic, backdrop any dream,
what Rosalind brought to her antic Arden,
a riddling place that questions all you ask,
full of shock, as in the primal exile garden
anything hidden it proves ready to unmask.
A forest moves, leads us on and eerily astray,
and shall forever come to take Macbeth away.

Long Ago Is Far Away

Long ago *is* far away
regarding time and space
for every passing day
loses a hopeless race,

removes the lasting trace
of dreams I had of you
with nothing to replace
what proved never true.

Space recedes like time
as the far away goes slow
in the way a cradle rhyme
will fade to the long ago

with nothing left to link
recall to a special place
for in but a single blink
full decades are erased.

So, by hour and expanse
thus vanishes your face
as if memory by trance
time and space unbrace.

A continuum disdains
whatever yearns to stay,
and loss alone remains
long ago and far away.

Mrs. Komodo in Mid-Scream

> "I need you to back me up in all matters."
> —to her husband

Mrs. Komodo, who never hid her aggravations,
literally rose like a red balloon virtually every morning
to snap and bark at her small children, innocent

and peering up bewilderedly at her gorgon hair,
serpentine, alive, almost radiating electric fission, creating
in her abuse a template in them of lifetime terror—

bursting harangues like shrieks of sexual frenzy
in former days used to call for exorcism, the freakazoid's
ballooning colon a sign of the devil's possession—

her hooting mouth a cardboard toilet paper tube
absorbing most of the blast of wet spittle rising like a fury
from rectal impaction, execrable, enema-deep,

a horn-mad sign, smelling of flatulence, bristling
eyes, methane-reeking barks, a flatographic tally of rancor
in the way it activated stretch receptors, digesta,

summoning hell itself! Wrath, a gasotransmitter
in releasing odors, emits a reeking far, far worse than smell.
Due to her gastrocolic howls, protruding eyes,

an inflation of her jumbo rectum as she shrieked,
this woman never looked homelier, her brain a prison bread
of worminess, damp as some mephitic swamp.

And all the while, in their immaculate innocence,
the children sat to the shrill and feel the lubricant, the eggy
stench, the noise *which they would never forget!*

Elias Pennebaker Hated Bitterns

He drove an old black 1932 Essex
and didn't mind its dense black smoke because
while it poured from the exhaust,

it blew toward the farty-smelling marsh
he rumbled by every morning in hat four-door sedan
with its defective latch on his side

to mercilessly plague the bitterns,
which woke him early up every morning. "Goddam
winged ferrets," he cursed, yanking

on his boots to take up his chores.
He had a small chicken farm in Truro. "You cause
as much a damned ruckus getting up,"

snarled Mrs. P. lying abed, muttering
into the pillow. "That cackle I hear? Does a hen
lay an egg standing up or sitting?"

he would angrily snap at the Mrs.
when she told him to just back off and leave them be
and that he made too much of a fuss.

"'Parently lying down's the answer!"
snapped Eli and slammed the screen door, leaving
to check the nests, clutches, perches,

often lifting hens, stacking eggs (never more
than five layers high) in paper crates to load the car,
the echo of his wife loud as the birds.

(She once made herself inconspicuous
in the hen house to check, gleefully hoping to prove
Eli wrong—but he was right: *standing*.)

She was bossy. "Empty the culch, Epo!"
"Use the dooryard!" when he came in with dirty boots
she'd yell. "Put 'em down thu cellah!"

The distinctively weird mating call
of the stakedriver—American bittern—a shy, swamp-
dwelling bird, sounds though someone

were sharply driving a hardwood stake
into the tight frozen ground, and it wakened Pennebaker
every morning. What was that damned

old sound like anyway? A hydro pump?
Water drippin'? Ol' pipes googlin'? *"A toilet plunger!"*
shouted out the chicken farmer. "Ayuh!

Crazy eyes, crazy beaks, crazy noises!
Ayuh!" he would cry, exulting, hoping the Mrs. heard,
starting the engine his smoking old car,

belching black exhaust, the left door
badly wobbling as he drove past the farty-smelling marsh
and booming—*honking?*—creatures!

Salem, 1692

It was precisely the educated men
who voted hanging for witchcraft,
scholars in black hats and degrees
condemning souls evil and daft,

Puritan divines snooping the town
who pressing them flat with stones,
shrived them of their sulfurous sin
by crushing their skin and bones

to confess, raising a central gibbet,
to dispatch them on Gallows Hill,
as an intellectual's way to prohibit
any more diabolical tricks. To kill

was the best way to prevent a witch
from caw-cawing like demon rooks,
and all could quote with perfect pitch
sanction to do so in learned books.

Knowledge can be a precarious tool.
for it sanctions the righteous need
in an erudite fool to establish a rule
by whatever he has chosen to read

and it took but nine arrogant judges
to vouchsafe fine learning a fraud
and show academics with grudges
prove devils while playing at God.

Aiken Colcord's Tributary Meal

Old Aiken Colcord who headed out by skiff
to shoot a seal or two down by Matinicus way off the coast
always brought along with his .33-55 rifle

a bag of apples, crisp juicy Hubbardstons
that had a sweet light plum and even grape flavor, a touch
of something herbal, "nonesuches," lunch

now that the Mrs. had died. Smutty Nose—
the Maine coast is peppered with tiny islands just like his,
Ten Pound, Resolution, Burial, Ministerial,

Grog, Winter, The Ark, Widow, Little Duck—
was where they had spent their lives, farming, selling milk
to Butter Island and vegetables to cottages

across to Eggemoggin Reach and Isle au Haut,
but now that he was alone, he set out for seals. She was seventy-six,
smoked, a clay pipe upside down, loved warmth,

so, it was ironic, her passing in the dead of winter,
just after, to meet her needs, they had both gone to Thomaston
where opening his canvas purse he bought in cash

a solid Monitor 81, worthy successor to their low
wood-burning Clarion stove, which could take a full half-cord,
two-foot sticks. They sang, "Throw Out the Life Line,

Someone Is Sinking Today" from an old hymnal.
"She faces east and west," tutmouthed old Reuel had pronounced
when asked at the grave site by the minister

(called in) which direction it was his island faced,
Methodists preferring head to west to civilize the ground,
but for the old man who knew seals by wind

the point was moot. "Spruces facing either side
go thin and grow upwards," he said. He dug the grave by hand,
ten hours. Elspeth had been scalded by hot water,

spilled, with flour employed to dry up the fluid
from the blisters, but in vain. There is no record of any doctor
being called. To keep his mind steadily off death,

he took his rifle and apples and set off sealing
and bagged two, to sell and in Spring to repaint the cow barn
with a mixture of seal oil and red ocher to compose

a rugged barn paint able to defy, and then some,
the elements a Down East gale could throw at you in November,
tough as cormorants or "shags" that sailed the sea.

It was now all about blubbering the seals for oil,
which brought market cash over at Frenchboro and by Monhegan,
and sales to local Grindles, Cliffords, and Snows.

Winter had set in. His aim was true. Luck helped.
"Keep well hidden," he told himself, waiting. "Seals are smart.
They can discern shadows and count up to five."

By the stove stood Reuel, munching a Nonesuch,
content, feeling the stove draw swell as the January wind
howled above the chimney as in a very hot pan

he seared two seal flippers with island aromatics,
garlic, carrots, green onions, and maple syrup, the very meal
of all on Smutty Nose Island his wife most loved,

seeing to it that he set out two plates, two chairs,
and two small pieces of delicious seal meat as fervently sweet
as the hot curling smoke of Elspeth's clay pipe.

Henry Thoreau and the Wilderness

> "Have you have ever been out in the great alone?"
> —Robert W. Service

No, Henry neither liked nor accepted
the derogatory attitudes toward "wilderness" in the Bible
where, symbolic antidote to civilization,

prayers were wrested. Where the experience
of God's holy presence is difficult for most people to find,
he never failed to find it in the weald

and the wild, entering the woods as if
penetrating a woman, believing in the passion it held for him.
That was singularly prayer for him.

"My heart is a remnant white pine, beating
with sap, my hemlock hands as good as any tree." Solitude
filling his frontier head, he knew the God

he needed was in wilderness which was never
the sign of unhappiness or estrangement. Hunters become
merely predators in the way godly prayers

are too often commonly prayed on knees.
Hebrews trooped through the wilderness, always parched
for Jeremiah, Isaiah, Moses, where devils

are encountered, where one is cruelly put to the test,
saints sorely tempted, where angels are required to minister to one,
a Zin of strife, friction, discord, variance, disgrace,

and fear, with no prosperity found, only harshness
and isolation. Henry knew better. "In Wildness is the preservation
of the World," he proudly wrote. Our soul is soil.

Antarctica

At minus-70 degrees air bears the quality of fire.
its pointed light cruel, sharp and white like wire

with a weird edema that any football player feels
open to the thwack of sourest irons, bluest steels.

When stillness is absolute, sounds are magnified,
with noise as clear as silver bells and never pied.

Quiet yields to kinds of sounds it actually invites,
which in an acquiescent sense gives up its rights.

There is a horror where whiteness never speaks,
where in the freezing footsteps give off squeaks

like a bitten rabbit's shriek or a sound you hear
as a salmon is stripped by an eviscerating bear.

To reckon stillness only fools can try to name.
Silence has a width that nothing sane can tame.

A rarefied light in a fundament of brutal cold,
tearing one's eyes with sight of light white gold,

demands like plague absence of human form
with death predictable, and mystery the norm.

A rose-tinted promise with orange shadows,
with ice like a sky of a shimmering primrose

ceding to aqua blue shadows of night in day,
is merely a cruel game the glacial puts in play

eerily pretending you are safe and all is well
for here the biting frost is fire and fire is hell.

That din, loud tumult, that furor that you hear
inside your head that so magnifies your fear?

It is merciless quiet sound actually invites,
which, by acquiescence, has given up its rights.

the frozen horror where whiteness never speaks,
where in gelid silence footsteps give off squeaks

as loudness in a nightmare wakes you from a dream
and Arctic silence quietly swallows up your scream.

Watch the Skies

A hunter's ability to read a "sky map"
is an essential skill—above ice, the sky turns a pale white,
whereas above open water it is dark—

but in the Arctic wilds of sculpting winds
a palette of Chinese violet streaking off to tails of fearful gray,
in riot, inspires nothing at all of radiance

but true fear. No deep searches are further
called for but only the need to flee to ferret out a fort of snow
as a matter of life and death, for storms

spoiling up with black claws late in the day
tinged with a tornadic green boiling out of varying violet
can suddenly tear you off the gelid tundra

like an avenging eagle to bite out your eyes,
its talons widening the closer it comes to snatch and claw you
like turncoat-colored ribbons of the skies.

The LGTBQIA2S+ Rag

> "I accept reality and dare not question it."
> —Walt Whitman

Normalize all the men in skirts and men in dresses.
Normalize stylish she-male and he-males' tresses.
Normalize all the modern interchangeable couples.
Normalize all the troupes and groups of throuples.
Normalize those who use any holes for receptacles.
Normalize folks with doubtful tits and dead testicles.
Normalize all the three-ways, triads, bi-ads, x-ads.
Normalize naiads, groping orts and sorts, and dyads.
Normalize the endless parade of Venusian varieties.
Normalize all butches, femmes, and their satieties
Normalize all pansies, nancies, poofters, bussies.
Normalize the aunties, daddies, twinks, and hussies
Normalize every foix and futch, the heteroflexibles.
Normalize tomgirls, femboys, sexual incorrectibles.
Normalize LGTBQIA2S + any she- and he-things.
Normalize all the indefinables sporting gay wings.
Normalize every stunt of pumping, pimping, felching.
Normalize every act of humping, shrimping, belching.
Normalize all trans-athletes, normalize every fetish.
Normalize each soul hermaphroditish and coquettish.
Normalize every quack, queen, queer, and cuspidor.
Normalize every parade of fairy, fruit and fructidor.
Normalize fluid, questioning. intersexual renderings.
Normalize wemen, woemen, and all new genderings
Normalize two-spirit, three-spirit, four-spirit, five.
Normalize every invert, obvert, upvert, pervert alive.

God's Mother

Fabrizio rolled up the sky
from one edge to the other
and what he saw beyond was
God and his ancient mother.

Nothing of cerulean blue
colored the distant zone,
a universe merely of vapor
and a single silver throne,

occupied by the Creator
staring down at the Earth
and by his shoulder stood
she who'd given him birth.

A bleak heath soon appeared,
under mists blowing in gusts
breeding in doubtful Fabrizio
no end of vaulting mistrusts

about who ruled the universe
and the miasma in which it sat
and whether, given this woman,
a Creator was begot or begat.

A road crept like an adder
throughout the cloudy murk
where a cloud of unknowing,
as he stood fairly berserk,

told Fabrizio in the chaos
with nothing at all aligned
that the brume around him
all took place in his mind,

that he had but fashioned,
just like his very own name,
the murk of his own confusion
—in order to shift the blame

and elsewhere to put the fault,
as a mental patient's inclined
when called upon to explain
the personal defects of mind—

to assign the chaos he saw
(and spare himself any bother
and the Creator he feared)
to God's very own mother,

the formal cause of all trouble,
(with ease the guilty can switch)
and lay all psychological rubble
at the feet of one ruling bitch.

Dead Alive
a sonnet

Thermopylae, the Alamo, Little Big Horn,
defeats that carry now the aura of success,
proved men, ready with courage to caress
death, counted fear of sacrifice with scorn
who far preferred dying, living to outrival,
to join eternity in the twilight of the gods,
choosing heroism against impossible odds
to avoid the disgrace of the sin of survival.
Memorials rise strictly for the dead alone,
tombs to mark the butchered and the slain,
for mourners love to weep and hug in pain
and shun remnant soldiers who come home.
The vanquished achieve gallantry's height.
It is the fallen alone who continue to fight.

We All Die at the Perfect Moment

We all die at the perfect moment,
Death has his way of making sure.
No reason to cause a huge foment
by the drama of pleading for more

of life, citing previous component
of how your days transpired before
or finding the reaper an opponent
merely hell-bent on keeping score,

as your passing's but an atonement
for the full accumulations you bore
that exacts in a formal bestowment,
no matter how much you implore

by way of functional employment,
what time, now defeated, forswore,
with nothing to do with enjoyment
as you proceed to the final encore.

It is futile to seek a postponement,
in spite of what you may deplore,
for we die at the perfect moment
since life and death have rapport

who work an ideal deployment.
Light darkness will never restore.
Be resigned to life-long torment
but not *indeterminable* civil war.

Culinary Christmas

Lobsters taken green
from a cold briny sea
served up piping hot
in flaming red shells

with glistening sheen
fat, steaming and free
straight from the pot
inside me ring like bells.

Jocasta Hockey's Illness

Jocasta Hockey's illness, I thought, was a substitute
for the bohemianism that frightened her. When Luther believed
that purpose of the Divine Will is to crucify our will,

was he not making us directionless and forced to seek
action by way of countermanding voices that whisper in our ears?
I have often wondered if baleful schizophrenia is not,

deep down, a mental need, exclusive of the will,
to *feel* something, *hear* something, wildly to break through
the anesthesia of dull living, to prove to that person

that she wasn't just asleep. A profound if inexplicable
refusal to march in step. Something even working against
one's own self-interest, an anxious life-affirming glee

by the subconscious to "selve." A weird temptation
that even the most *well-adjusted* person feels at various points.
Madman Nietzsche offers thoughts along these lines

where he writes of polarities of the Apollonian
(a rationalist paradigm that fought the havoc of her life)
versus the Dionysian (a primordial celebration

of the dark, the wild, even the irrational). Jocasta
may be actually in rebellion, so to speak, against her demons,
to try to free itself as an act of existential defiance,

and, who knows, maybe identify herself with courage?
I felt it in her wish to kiss that day we sat together on the roof
when I said, "It may sound weird, but who knows,

how far the mind will take us, working as an antidote
to the wholesome, antiseptic doldrums of sanity? Dostoevsky
in his *Notes from Underground* speaks directly

to this point, insisting we often work against ourselves
as an existence assertion. When Aquinas went and defined man
fully as "a rational animal," was he not also half wrong?

What else are "voices" we hear but whispered offerings
suggestions we strive to keep our wills from being crucified,
hoping that by the direction of our will the *avant-garde*

in us will kick in to overcome any fear or terror so that
you, Jocasta Hockey, in your crazy daring beauty can finally
kiss me fully on the lips without a fickle fit of fear!

Ethiopian Food

Narcotic chat over,
a banana ensete meal so red
our bright black chef

served, a smoky cover
from an oily noog in a bed
of tiny grain called teff,

and, very like a drover
mixing finger millet, said,
"Hot! Make you deaf!"

as a heady scent of clover
with hints of beer with bread
struck a vivid treble clef,

and I lapped it up like Rover
wolfing down each scarlet shred
'til nothing more was left.

Bird Beaks

To sharpen its bill, indubitably, is a bird's first obligation
to itself, its pecking shovel for food, a bold essential tool,

a weapon, a sword, a spade, a hoe, both muzzle and nib,
its key to freedom, the denial of which is to cede power

to hawks, raptors. Tacitus, who hated power and found
in it a horrible denial of freedom, a seedbed of cruelty

and evil of every sort, constantly saw omens in birds
by way of their efficiencies, not a one more important

than to sharpen and shine its beak to a cutting blade
for point precision by stropping it on limbs for health,

fast-shifting it side to side barber-wise in a natural jib
to eat, to fight, to live avian life by fabricating wealth.

Merle Haggard Was a Wuss About His Mama

"There's no man in the world
More bound to [his] mother…"

"If my son were my husband, I should freelier
rejoice in that absence wherein he won honor
than in the embracements of his bed where
he would show most love."
—Coriolanus 5.3.157–8, 1.3, 2–5

Merle Haggard was a wuss about his Mama:
into every maudlin song she pokes her face.

Had he undergone some childhood trauma
which this yokel could not mentally erase,

or was it but typical hillbilly melodrama
squidbilly-sung to make the smarmy case

that he was just a simple country farmer
who, after a public penitentiary disgrace,

hoped to prove by his heart turned calmer
hayseed fans would quicker him embrace,

moaning all his songs like an embalmer
pleading for a bit of extra bullshit grace?

Of any Daddy in the Haggard diorama
one finds, queerly, not a single a trace,

as if in that odd family cryptogramma
he was relegated to some hiding place.

No redneck for me can be a charmer.
Okie Oedipus was just waste of space.

Stavrogin *et Cie*

> "Put sixteen girls on a stage and it's everybody—
> the world. Put sixteen boys and it's nobody."
> —George Balanchine

Ballet is all about unspecified emotions
and in that sense is part of a lie, but one scrutability in an art
full of them—Balanchine was ever coy

about any meanings his fey dances had—
was how young girls, "baby ballerinas," fed his morbid interest
in yearning for a beauty he did not possess,

quiet orphan girls used to displacements,
thin, needy, pretty frail ingenues who always got up to dance
when music played and poetry was spoken.

They each became his milk-white Galatea.
He married Tamara Geva at the age of fifteen, gave Toumanova
an expensive watch when she was twelve,

went weak in the knees for the teenage girls,
mostly children of Russian emigres in Paris, seducing them all
for their girlish innocence to go on *pointe*

—a straight male in that wispy wayward world
is a wolf among sheep—but when Suzanne Farrell appeared,
the epitome of a juvenile bantling cherub

sweet urchin, sexy brat, urchin, whippersnapper,
hoyden, and long-legged tomboy in white tights all at once,
he went mad with love, virtually losing all control

in an obsession, forgetting all his four wives
and other fond baby loves, Irina Baronova, Tamara Toumanova,
Tatiana Riabouchinska. Russian men notoriously

share a lusty *frisson* for early teenage girls,
Goncharov, Nabokov, Balanchine, and even outright criminals
who killed and mummified them, true perverts

like Stavrogin who in Dostoevsky's *The Devils*
foully describes in a confessional letter—the scorbutic chapter
"At Tikhon's," censored, only later published—

a lengthy and detailed self-admiring document,
to taking advantage of downtrodden despairing Matryosha,
a vulnerable eleven-year-old girl, and then waiting

and listening in the next room, keen for details
and aware of what she's doing, hot for specified emotions,
as she proceeds in despair to hang herself,

a girl used to displacements, telling her mother
that she has "killed God." I find it ironically apropos that Stavrogin's
suicide by garrote—read the passage—is balletic.

A Trial of the Body Is a Test of the Soul

A trial of the body is a test of the soul.
Climb to the exact top of a mountain
to find, and so make, yourself whole.
A drive within the heart of a fountain
attests to the glory of the spout above.
Reach when you run to divine a spirit
that proves in you a speed to behove,
axes around which both drives pivot.
Muscle function aligns with thought
as dreams teach hope by what we do.
Joy of the inner self is regally bought
when a body's display affirms it true.
Both soul and body conjoin at the root.
Lewis and Clark trod the last mile on foot.

Big White Hunter

> "So back we turned to where the big tusker lay, and
> I felt proud indeed as I stood by the immense bulk
> of the slain monster and put my hand on the ivory."
> —Theodore Roosevelt, *African Game Trails* (1910)

So cruel
Immorally
Killing an elephant
Dying with a shrill trumpet
Accompanied by hacks and lackeys
Hunting heavy game with his Holland .500-.450
Fat Theodore Roosevelt on Mount Kenia moving forward
Sneaking upon it (with his armed guides) like any coward
Saw the bull with heavy tusks and never thrifty
In glorified boots and chic khakis
Shot it again to pump it
Typically arrogant
For novelty
A fool

Movie Star

A movie star is a person
who transcends any role that is played.
Do not work at emoting.

Be merely who you are.
Play the very same role all the time,
basically, stupidly floating.

A star simply shines in a part,
not interfering with her natural gift,
solely her reason for gloating.

Tenement Stairs

Echo is a color
as much as noise,

musty oil a sound
as much as a smell,

as fright climbs up
in a terrified soul.

My N.Y.C. walk-up
stank of darkness,

death-old treads
creaking cracking

narrow landings
damp hollow air

splintered steps
with loud footfall

worn down smooth
on fevered wood

by odd immigrants
trudging to work

in tiny sweatshops
dropping below

holding filthy walls
windowless stalls

inhaling dust-filled
rat-ball sediment

unventilated, mostly
in windowless shafts

stairwells all dark
and thick with dust.

Pink, Blue, Purple

Rock Hudson, who was gay,
was not good acting epicene man;

in *Pillow Talk* in odd display,
he came across as a Dapper Dan,

effortfully feigning to be fey
to trick a cutie catch-as-catch-can,

(a woman played by Doris Day)
predictably virile by scripted plan

in scenes calling to act that way
tall, dark, rugged, handsome, tan,

all decked out in manly array
(opting in secret for a chiffon caftan?),

yet one may ask by such display
was he fighting a type to avoid a ban,

and in the process critics allay,
of the gay homosexual ilk and clan,

but, while doing himself, betray
simply to appease every movie fan

for he came across in every way
as fully male, playing male dead pan,

in every last scene he had his say
from a movie's end to the way it began,

recalling *Twelfth Night*, that play
where a male portrays an actual woman,

Viola, robed as a whimsical stray,
who, in turn, struts about just like a man.

Pink, Blue, Purple: of the trey,
who may then say what cannot be or can?

For each sex leads the other astray:
if one is more, why, the other's less than!

It is certain alone by every survey,
that gender is—front and rear—a sedan.

Magnificent Sumo Wrestlers

Size is never not a forum
of what dimension promises.

No bow isn't generous
and the way dignity offers itself,

respect for old tradition—
—fair play—is already a victory.

The sport is quite simple,
just a few seconds and the winner

is walking from the ring,
peacefully, as before the match.

Contestants have no hatred
in their eyes, provoke no quarrels.

They accept their destiny.
Beefy bulk is an added generosity,

a waistline, burgeoning with
cheery chubbery is bounty in itself,

and, as every oval opens
wide, it, by definition, only invites.

Green Monster

Her beauty was deceiving
because she threw away goodness
the way every plant or tree

dispenses with green light
while absorbing colors red and blue,
that in free fall humans see,

for the red she loved of sin,
the blue she caused in others by dint
of all the lies she gave so free.

Ghoulography

> "There is aggression implicit in every use of a cameras—
> to photograph people is to violate them."
> —Susan Sontag

Ms. Phosphorus Gelmitz. a feminist, investing herself
in her photographs, recognized money where barmies sat. Shooting them
became a joy pluperfect in its ease, for well she knew,

secretly—no doctrine!—you just pointed and clicked.
Come on, a *machine* does it! She roamed 42nd St. looking for surprises.
All photographs are stolen—clipped, exist by theft,

quietly, the way ghee brightens a chicken biriani.
There is a prurience in exploitation, the tip-toing way a voyeur in her heart
goes squealing with delight in her silent snatching.

Cartier-Bresson often hid behind a tree, with squirrels.
He liked the smallest cameras, an M3 Leica out of his pocket, no gadgets,
a 50-millimeter lens. Equipment brought attention

and prevented the quick draw. He never used a light meter,
the way discretion would not, scavenging in people's privacy for money.
Avedon in his prissiness *boasted* that, with photography,

all art was invasive. "That's the property of a work of art,"
he claimed. (His flaw was self-congratulation.) But the question
 remains,
is photography art? No, it is essentially hunting, banging

through jungle to bring down prey: hide, spy, shoot, kill, pose,
stand on the victim's head. Garry Winogrand, Danny Lyon, Robert
 Frank,
all should have worn hunting camouflage, mimicry

and break-up, camo patterns to deceive, which is why
Cartier-Bresson loathed color photography: it shone too bright a
 light
on what, from perches, was silently being filched.

A failure of decency is behind all robbery. Shoplifting,
pilferage, holdups, appropriation. Bold embezzlement fits a
 darkroom
to a T. "It's what I've never seen before that I recognize,"

was the way intruder Diane Arbus, resorting to paradox,
explained her infringements, taking immodest pictures of broken
 lives
like nutball Ms. Gelmitz, following in her hairy wake,

roaming the purlieus of circuses, psycho wards, bagnios,
funny farms, Texas snake handling shows, sanitariums, rubber
 rooms,
dragging along her medium-format Rolleiflex like a gun.

Wet Blankets

Black walnut trees all sadly drop
their leaves so swiftly that they're bare
when other trees go flashing color;

it's the case with butternuts, too,
so parsimonious with display it seems
they clearly prefer naked dolor.

Locusts retain their chlorophyll,
so are green until the leaves drop off
offering up to no one a display.

Why these shedding variations
in the quixotic dendrological world?
It would take a wizard to say.

The ash tree and the chestnut
always rashly race to drop their leaves,
and the perverted sycamore

does not fully shed its leaves
until cold midwinter when no living soul
looks for any color anymore.

Hackberry, hickory, and holly,
very like the rude live oaks in summer,
all lose their leaves in spring.

So, why do we expect of nature
in the way that she presents herself
cyclic logic in a living thing?

The color we see is the color
from that part nature coldly rejects,
and but feigns its claim to love,

to favor, to boast, to broadcast,
No, any disappointment in leaves
is surely as below as up above.

Greta Garbo

A face is never a mask.
Garbo was allowed to subjectivize her parts,
flat out refusing to be a type

in which she lost herself.
A truly great actress, in a sense, is never one
and does not act or hype

but reveals natural magic,
portraying the original liberating force *she is*,
a chevron, not a stripe.

The expressions she achieved
were subtle. Her personality was her art,
a perfect fruit, perennially ripe.

Twin

for Shenandoah and Shiloh
Christmas 2019

As a noun it indicates a couple or a pair,
but as a verb, unnervingly, it can mean

to part, severe, sunder, in the odd way
that to cleave means, by hacking clean,

to part, severe, sunder, the very way
that it equally means to cling together

as well as, perversely, to whack apart,
the antithesis of binding or to tether.

A prayer is when our girls separate
they do not divide but, splitting, state
twoness by birth is our blessed fate.

Limpet

Shorty Shea was steered by a beavering drive
not to know or learn and at school saw poems

as hated enemies in that, badly confounding him,
held secrets perfectly engineered to throw him,

and, so, whenever he had the chance, he sought
to scissor out any rhyme or jingle on any page,

a lunatic act in the fetid stalls of library toilets
he'd perform with an ugly, masturbatory rage.

He married a chinless girl whose genius uncle,
as cruel fate would have it, happened to write

the very kind of—in his case brilliant—poetry,
of the sort, mocking him, Shea cut out from spite!

Gangling, crabby mouth, sneering gristly nose,
spiky hair, he had the sour face of an intruder,

a low-born limpet, an ignoramus born to butle,
a prick in three parts: griper, growler, brooder.

He *demanded* that she willingly ditch her book,
swearing with a curse otherwise he'd force her,

and that if their two kids, a small boy and girl,
said a fucking poem he'd instantly divorce her!

Knowledge he could neither know nor learn
brought low his ego by lessening his height.

It was in his Irish ugliness that darkness won
over the defeating misery of all and any light.

Reverend Treat Is Laughing Again

> "The effects of [Treat's] preaching, it is said, was that his hearers were several times in the course of his ministry awakened and alarmed, and on one occasion a comparatively innocent young man was frightened nearly out of his wits, and Mr. Treat had to exert himself to make hell seem somewhat cooler to him."
> —Thoreau, *Cape Cod*

In far Eastham on old Cape Cod
Reverend Samuel Treat, passing odd,

was so loud whenever he spoke
that his Sunday sermons awoke

in terror and frightened the few
who'd sit quaking in their pew,

for his threatening caveats bold
received like a burning scold

gave every doctrine he preached
a dimension of added screech

and warnings as black as thunder
forced his flock to knuckle under,

for nothing quite serves the right
like a godly admonition of fright.

§

When storms on terrible nights
blow in like Nature's last rites

with wind gusts of evil scope
as contorted as twisted rope

vibrating walls and every rafter
like Satan in the hell hereafter,

timbers creaking and quaking
as if God's heaven forsaking,

all the village children in fear
and in pure panic turn an ear

to ask of their parents the cause
and be advised without pause,

(as in Eastham they still explain):
"Reverend Treat is laughing again."

Salt Herring

Elkanah, pulling on his old rubber gloves,
nodded once, north. "Yup," he spat, again,
"Yup. Truro was once called Dangerfield."
His cheeks were scarlet, scraggly his beard,

and with bony digits he was boxing fish,
salt herring. I'd been seeking directions,
traveling to take some photographs, and
he judged me overdressed, bundled up—

"First week in December? It's deer week.
Hell, you go walking the dunes like that,
you'll be shot"—slapping up the fillets
I was buying, all barrel cured and brined.

I'd interrupted him in the yard there
by Oyster Road (my map), filled with
wooden traps, red-and-white buoys,
a tangle of jungled nets, and a boat.

"Mind me askin' you what in tunket,
bedamned—mind the clammin' hoe afoot!—
you be takin' pictures *of* in the dunes?
Here, don't step on that goddam hay,

cause the damn cows wount eat it."
He held up a herring and wagged it.
"Eats real good with slumgullion
or what the Mrs. calls potato bargain.

You ever et it? Called lobscouse, too."
One hand robbed the other, working
in tandem, as he filled up fat one box
only to sling up another on the table.

"Old timers here cured 'em in the sun,
smoked 'em up blue, alder chips best,
strung them through the gills, sold 'em
a dozen on a stick. A string of herring

was priced, oh, about a dime back then.
Crowells, Nickersons, Stones, Bodfishes,
Hinckleys, Pells, old families all raised
on 'em to eat. Alewives, shads, whatever

you choose call 'em. Moonies. Sawbelly,
best eaten with boiled potatoes and beer.
Used to say, whosoever ate lots of herring
become over time so gol-darned tempered

to the nasty wee bones contained in 'em
it took a full day's work for 'em to get"
he laughed—"out of their underwear!"
I paid. "You go walking in the dunes

'bout now, December, first week or so,
like I say," he blew on his whit-flawed
fingers, "you *too* be found spread out,
kippered! Talkin' bout Dangerfield!"

Go Away!

We'd get along if she was shy
wouldn't speak up or even stir.

The trouble is, she doesn't try
to avoid me, as I try to do her.

Is such a plea a pie in the sky
to beg sometime not to recur,

who insists to stay, so to deny
that a pittance of peace occur?

But that is the show of the shy,
to depart, disappear, and defer,

not just stand by hopelessly nigh
in the way of some family cur

to argue once more to amplify
the feud and continue to spur

the spat and so to feign thereby
that we are the way we were?

Why a need to fucking reply
and perpetuate the longueur,

sticking around under my eye
playing the vicious saboteur?

That is never a mode of a guy,
only the way of a buffalo burr,

a crone to perpetually drop by,
an argumentative entrepreneur,

droning on with a hue and a cry,
with a brain dry as a jointed fir.

Goodbye, Xanthippe, good bye!
I had sooner a cold death prefer!

This Way to the Human Race

Wear on your feet the shoes of deceit.
Trim your trousers with cuffs of spite.
Sport your hat with a haughty conceit.
Show no regret to starvation or blight.
This way to the human race.

Select your choice of hypocrite hats.
Don the most insincere of your ties.
Let your implacable jacket and spats
match your penchant for telling lies.
This way to the human race.

Twirl as you walk a duplicitous cane.
If two-faced your smile, all the better.
If your gold links cause envious pain,
you've fulfilled your role to the letter.
This way to the human race.

Walk past the poor with utter contempt.
Flash your watch until their eyes hurt.
Of their own filthy fate feel fully exempt.
Let them suck on the cost of your shirt.
This way to the human race.

God Always Sees a Child Escapes a Massacre

> "The object of life is not to be on the side of the majority,
> but to escape finding oneself in the ranks of the insane."
> —Marcus Aurelius

God always sees a child escapes a massacre,
that strife in a rock fought world, immune to care, would kill it.
Moses was such a child, basketed in bulrushes

to be adopted and eventually to deliver his people.
So, too Jesus, taken to Egypt, to avoid the swords of Herod Antipas,
slaughtering innocents out of insane paranoia.

Athalia, daughter of King Ahab and Jezebel,
two maniacs, by royal fiat had forty-two princes quickly butchered
she saw as rivals, but one of them escaped,

one-year-old Joash who was hidden in a temple
through the care of a couple, the caring priest Jehoiada and his wife,
and, escaping, thrived to become king of Judah

to reign for forty years, after his grandmother Athalia,
the vengeful, was executed. If you believe you're free, no escape
is possible, yet. You are made free to be aware,

with God's grace, but they escape into consequences
who survive, as being born from the menacing threat one is forced
never to forget, reminded by default they live.

Alistair Thumb and Alison Space

Alistair Thumb and Alison Space
Kept their brat in a packing case
Alison Space and Alistair Thumb
One to wash its face, one to wash its bum
O, it's my turn now said Alison Space
To grab a washcloth and scrub its face
And it's my turn now said Alistair Thumb
To snatch my scrubcloth to wash its bum.

Alistair Thumb and Alison Space
Indifferent as to closed-in space
Alison Space and Alistair Thumb
Agreed on the application of navy rum
To Alison Space her devoted attends
Offered equal share in the dividends.
While her partner Alistair Thumb
Splashing its bottom made it hum.

Alistair Thumb and Alison Space
Finding in nurture an obstacle race
Alison Space and Alistair Thumb
Soon gave less to the brat than rum.
You nipped full half said Alison Space
Who gulping the rest left not a trace
Bugger the brat said Alistair Thumb.
Flat on the floor half deaf and dumb.

Alistair Thumb and Alison Space
Beside each other both out of place
Alison Space and Alistair Thumb
By furcating jobs made a zero sum.
Full attention—not a partial embrace—
Was an alien concept to Alison Space.
Same with zonked-out Alistair Thumb
Who gave up the brat in a legal scrum.

The Faces of Modigliani

It is said that no Modigliani woman
ever truly existed in life, but I saw one
one rainy night at La Bellevilloise,

long necked, a head oddly tipped,
cold mask-like with almond eyes, slits
really, that bravura contouring

of form, an arabesque flung out
like a coil of bluejacket's line, dropping
down bosom-less and resigned.

Modi put a pure pallor to his whites
with varnish. His black is blue, imposed
on green, the way an alcoholic

sees a morning sky. He never erred
when drawing very rapidly, never erased,
flouted no conventions with his dolls.

Alcohol marginalized him; better
to put paint to women from hazy dreams
with giraffe necks, squeezed eyes,

elongations brushed onto a canvas
while sipping absinthe, biting knobs of hash,
squinting, for slant eyes one never

sees except in the elemental sadness
that seems natural to the world of innocence,
even if stumbling out of a nightclub.

Mrs. Stakeknife

A wife who appropriates a child hates her spouse,
but empty-souled humans crave a power to fill it.
With the black calculating eyes of a shrew mouse,
she bides her time watching prey hoping to kill it.

Her long running dream is to see her rival dead,
for a husband of a possessive mother is a danger.
His freedom with a child causes ultimate dread.
She *delights* in the bristles of a rivalrous anger.

The Judge with the Gerbil IQ

Judge Clarence Thomas has $32 million worth of assets
by which he lives not by what he gives but what he gets.

Missing any facility for engagements in oral arguments,
his sole contribution to the bench basically is corpulence.

The demands of neither Logic nor Truth ever occur to him.
Few jurists on the Supreme Court rarely ever defer to him.

With barely one weak year of experience on the judiciary,
a goofball to whom law as concept is basically imaginary,

he was laughably nominated to the Supreme Court in 1991,
far less as a token black than an international figure of fun.

His billionaire friends send him on luxury trips they pay for
which is the primary reason on this high court he stays for.

He sits glum on the bench as ineffectual as a cement block,
paring his nails, yawning, farting, and staring at the clock,

planning to sail off to the Bahamas on some patron's dime
stretching out on shore with Ginny, having a glorious time

or zipping to Indonesia on all expenses-paid boondoggles
on extra super yachts with Texas billionaires and models

and then to fly home to find piles of many lobbyists' gifts
from those seeking patronage, the usual Washington stiffs.

Hoping we're as pig ignorant as he, banking so to trust us
with his criminal sloth, he should be called an—*Injustice!*

Asclepias Tuberosa

Mid-July sees the orange tavern closed,
its sweet flowers battered and ravaged,

sucked of hot nectar and discomposed
by a mad army of thirsty bees, savaged,

a crowd of drunkards on a tip-and-run,
their tiny faces tangerine cups, crazed

hopheads quaffing heady drinks in sun,
winging away by afternoon half-dazed,

soon to be back again only to discover,
rather like a Sunday in Puritan Boston,

try although they buzz about or hover,
premises are shut, no bar to get lost in.

Martin Buber Steals the Jerusalem Family Home of the Writer Edward Said

Martin Buber, that craven Jewish mouse,
author of the posturing book, *I and Thou*,
in 1948 moved into the old family house
of Edward Said, reciting the Israeli vow
that Jerusalem's for Jew's. "Why grouse?"
he asked. "Your house is my house now!

Haven't you read my sententious book?
I'm the living expert of mine and thine!
Go to some Arab bookshop, have a look.
Thou has rights, it is true, but I in kind
can legitimately grab by hook or crook
and claim by law 'What's yours is *mine*!'"

Face of a Rose of Sharon

The face of a Rose of Sharon flower looks a granny,
a long sharp white spinster nose poking out to scold,

the frilly, silly bunting of her bonnet shows her old,
though attempting to look young, a sneering nanny,

more croak than crocus, with that lavender uncanny
withering revealed within every tiny wrinkled fold.

Easy It Didn't Was

Shy Mr. Slutsky, a conservative, clutching his broad-brimmed flat hat,
crouched in tents to counsel us, never bold like the other scoutmasters,

and used to say, "Nothing should ever be done for the first time," fearful
of god knows what. Was it sage counsel or cowardice, the way he would

sequester himself in fearfulness? No stout Roman who ate baby dormice
dipped in honey and swallowed then whole like oysters ever felt that way!

He used to read the Sunday funnies to us whenever the weather was bad
or it was pouring, crowding on as we bivouacked, knee to knee, near me.

When he touched my bum, when we were alone, I suspected he thought that.
Why do people sacrifice the permanent for the satisfaction of the immediate?

I ask, because that question came to me about the behavior of the unbrave,
who in rare incautious moments uncharacteristically take a daring chance,

against all odds, passion garbling their principles like a person stuttering
and, blushing, dare a bad thing. As Milt Gross said, "Easy it didn't was."

To Morons Who Wastefully Leave Lights Burning

Waste is a way of stating by heedlessness
I am a phenomenon whose grasping and owning presence
—a boast, in fact—claims I won't be limited

by my absence. "Screw rules! *You* pay for it,"
squander mutters through a slovenly intemperance of mouth,
for by leaving all the lights on in the house

I not only awaken your weak, weeviling worries,
scold, but feel I philosophically let the light explore itself
while I seek other priggeries. Americanism

is about lavishness, misdisposing, like buyers
of organic goods love hemorrhaging money, their frittering
foolishness the vanity of umbrella-heads who spend

their lives in a blight of insubstantial darkness.
Prodigality is a *destination*! To have no such regard wobbles
in its dissipation through rubble, waste, trash,

in the way of frivoling neglect, for what is spent
on a splurge points to a future need for what has been lost,
as light is sadly spilt on nothing that's observed.

Indians of Arizona

The eagles rise,
wings swoop high,

a southwest sun
in the azure sky,

an antelope priest
chants by drum

by a tall saguaro
as deserts thrum.

Maricopa, Navajo,
Cocopah, Papago,

Apache, Yavapai,
Mojave, Hualapai,

Chemehuevi, Pima,
Havasupai, Yuma,

Shipaulovi, Hopi.
Paiute, Moencopi.

The eagles rise,
wings swoop high,

a southwest sun
in an azure sky,

an antelope priest
chants by drum

by a tall saguaro
as deserts thrum.

There Exists That Rare Freedom

There exists that rare freedom
that only comes from limits. Study the way,
say, Goya put war between frames

to show us license can murder,
draw a bead on how excesses imprison but
in a perverse way don't contain

the wrath our own discrete skulls,
a box with a lesson, a barrier with a lecture,
daily would restrain, curb, suppress.

The Nutcracker rats were happier
out of Clara's fervid dreams, most notably the
overreaching Mouse King

slaughtered in his tracks to music.
I could point to Caesar and rivers he crossed.
Whatever curbs, caps, contains.

None gains control over license
unless he learn that the conflict and battle
that we exact in a waddling way

exceeds what vouches to enable
us by mere restriction. Curtailment begs to see
us succeed only by what we cede.

www.ingramcontent.com/pod-product-compliance
Lightning Source LLC
LaVergne TN
LVHW012246070526
838201LV00090B/131